HIDDEN HISTORY *of the* MINNESOTA RIVER VALLEY

HIDDEN HISTORY *of the* MINNESOTA RIVER VALLEY

ELIZABETH JOHANNECK

THE History PRESS

Published by The History Press
Charleston, SC 29403
www.historypress.net

Back cover image: Painting by Minnesota's Grandpa Moses, Arnold Kramer (1882–1976). Entitled *Rohlik Threshing Rig*. Currently part of the Elizabeth Johanneck collection.

Unless otherwise noted, all photos are by or from the collection of Elizabeth Johanneck, Minnesota Country Mouse Folk Blog.

First published 2010
Second printing 2012
Third printing 2013

Manufactured in the United States

ISBN 978.1.59629.881.1

Library of Congress Cataloging-in-Publication Data

Johanneck, Elizabeth.
Hidden history of the Minnesota River Valley / Elizabeth Johanneck.
p. cm.
ISBN 978-1-59629-881-1
1. Minnesota River Valley (S.D. and Minn.)--History--Anecdotes. 2. Minnesota River Valley (S.D. and Minn.)--History, Local--Anecdotes. 3. Minnesota River Valley (S.D. and Minn.)--Biography--Anecdotes. I. Title.
F612.M4J58 2010
977.6'3--dc22
2010012977

Lovingly Dedicated to
Geoff, Adriane & Jojo
&
Kasey & Jayvyn

—In Memory of Ed Michael—

Contents

Contents

Introduction

It occurred to me early on in the process of writing about the history of the Minnesota River Valley that it was important to begin by referencing history on a larger scale in order to help map out events leading to the cataclysmic social changes that took place in the valley during the nineteenth century.

History is often written in subjective terms and themes, and heroes are determined by which side of the story you're on. I'd love to be the exception, but the truth is, if it hadn't been for the guidance of my friend and mentor Audrey Kletscher Helbling, a writer from Faribault, Minnesota, this book would have consisted of pages of personal opinion and very little substance. History is fascinating, entertaining and surprising, with all sorts of valuable life lessons if we're willing to learn them.

Hidden History of the Minnesota River Valley took on a life of its own, attracting stories I had never heard before and presenting me with familiar stories in which astonishing facts had been left out through the sin of omission. I've tried to present a dispassionate and more complete picture of river valley history than I am accustomed to, weaving together bits and pieces of information gathered through interviews and a vast array of sources. I have striven for accuracy, having to rely, in some cases, on the folklore of the valley.

My apologies go out to the courageous women of the Minnesota River Valley who are not fairly represented in this collection of tales, for surely their stories warrant a book of their own.

I am grateful to my brilliant and beautiful mother, Marie, who encouraged my creativity and taught me to always do the toughest job first. I have my old dad, Lenus, to thank for the gift of his storytelling and the hours he spent with me doing just that. I must also thank my siblings, Philip, Steve, Kevin, Bob, Jeff, Annie, Pete and Danny, for the gift of childhood memories, including those golden Sunday picnics in the Minnesota River Valley.

Early on in my life, I was blessed with a best friend, Cindy Bernardy Lavin. She, along with her steady husband Bill, shared the ups and downs of my life and encouraged me in all my creative endeavors. I have, for decades, appreciated Cindy's gift for embellishment, prompting Bill to occasionally ask, "Now, Cindy, did that *really* happen?" I owe a special thanks to Bill for providing copies of the letters preserved by the Granite Falls Historical Society for the chapter on J. Edgar Hoover.

I am constantly grateful for my wanderlust-afflicted friend, Melanie Dunlap, without whom the Minnesota Country Mouse Folk Blog would not exist, and for her husband, Dave, who encourages our outings.

Thank you to my dear friends Luci Eichten, a grounding influence in my life, and Monica Fischer, who graciously allowed me to use images from her Grandma Angie Bergen's antique postcard collection. It was Monica, after all, who taught me to fly my freak flag.

It's been a challenging task to write a book on a deadline, so I thank my supervisor Sarah Thapa, from Park Nicollet Methodist Hospital in the Third Party Follow-up Department, for helping me schedule the time to write. I am grateful, also, to my co-workers, Annie, Mark, Katie, Jenny, Shirley, Paul, Cindy, Jim and Robbie, for weathering my panic and pulling my weight when I wasn't there to do it. Their encouragement has been priceless.

A special thank-you must be afforded to Terry Sveine of New Ulm, Minnesota, and Audrey Kletscher Helbling for their literary contributions to the book.

I am grateful to historians Scott Larson and Gary Revier of Redwood Falls, Minnesota, for providing information and photographs about their region. Thank you, Gary Anderson, for introducing me to the colorful Minnesota River Valley character Judge Theodore Weiland.

I am honored and grateful that Chief Ernest Wabasha and his courageous wife, Vernell, took the time to meet with me, enabling me to see that some of the history of the Minnesota River Valley I learned as a child was upside-down.

Many thanks to kindred spirit Big Carl Lithander for accompanying me on this journey.

To those of you I have neglected to mention but have played an important part in the writing of this book, please forgive me, and I thank you.

BONES

Dear Diary,

When I drove into the Minnesota River Valley in southwestern Minnesota last week on my way to the family farm, I recalled a conversation I had with a member of the Lower Sioux tribe from Morton back in the early 1990s while I was living here.

He said the tribe was still trying to recover the remains of their relatives who had been hanged in Mankato in the largest mass-execution in our country's history, after the U.S. Dakota Conflict of 1862. I tried to imagine what that must feel like. After all, my relatives are all neatly buried in well-marked graves where I can visit and leave a handful of wildflowers when the spirit moves me.

In spite of its heartbreaking past (after all, you can feel the sadness in the trees and the banks of the river) I thought about how wonderful it is that the Minnesota River Valley is here so we can study its history, learn its lessons

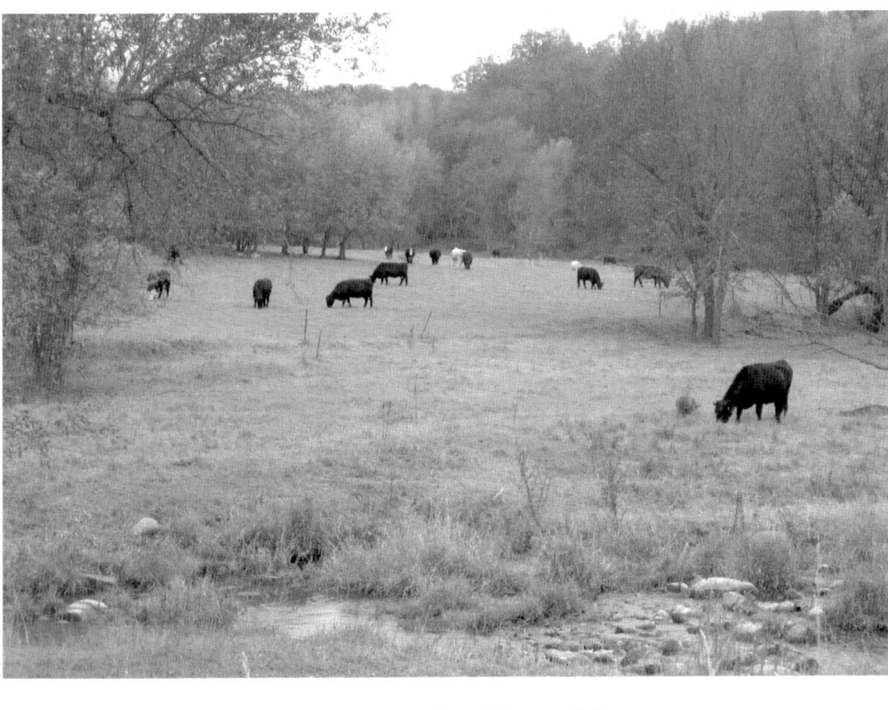

Cows grazing in the Minnesota River Valley near Morton, Minnesota.

and photograph stunning vistas. And thanks to the Dakota tribes, we have an increase in employment at their casinos. It turns out that gambling is an activity that a lot of people from near and far enjoy. Who knew?

My friend Melanie and I always say that the most interesting people live in the river valley. It's a fact we are especially aware of when we visit its coffeehouses, gift shops and restaurants. It inspires music, writing and art.

The valley is also popular with the motorcycle crowd who can tour from the east end of the state to the west on the winding and wooded Minnesota River Valley National Scenic Byway. We are blessed.

This gorgeous river valley doesn't have a bad season, and unlike some of us, it looks good all year round.

Still, I can't help wondering. Did they ever get their bones back?

—Minnesota Country Mouse

Fort Snelling

Birthplace of Minnesota and the Dakota

My friend Angie and I allowed ourselves to be picked up by a couple of forty-something rock-and-rollers for a ride to Fort Snelling in Minneapolis. It was quite a ride. The music was ear-splitting, and Angie and I sat in the back seat of the van, observing a whole lot of air guitar and head banging. We slid our eyes at each other, trying not to laugh out loud at these old boys.

The point of our trip was to attend an open house in a part of the fort not typically made available to the public, giving us the chance to step behind the veil at the Upper Post. The free tour was designed to raise public awareness of old buildings in desperate need of preservation.

I was surprised to see how dilapidated these historic structures were. I firmly believe in the preservation of historic architecture, but this fort is not without its duplicitous past. I could feel it in the air. When it comes to history, it is imperative to remember *all* of it and not pick and choose only the parts we care to remember.

These buildings, from the earliest part of the 1800s, are some of the oldest in the state and should be considered for preservation. The round tower is the oldest man-made structure in the state. Imagine my surprise when I discovered there were those who thought the buildings should be removed. What kind of people would feel that way?

Alexander Ramsey, territorial governor of Minnesota, said in 1849, "Let us save that which is interesting in the fleeting registers of the day, and which

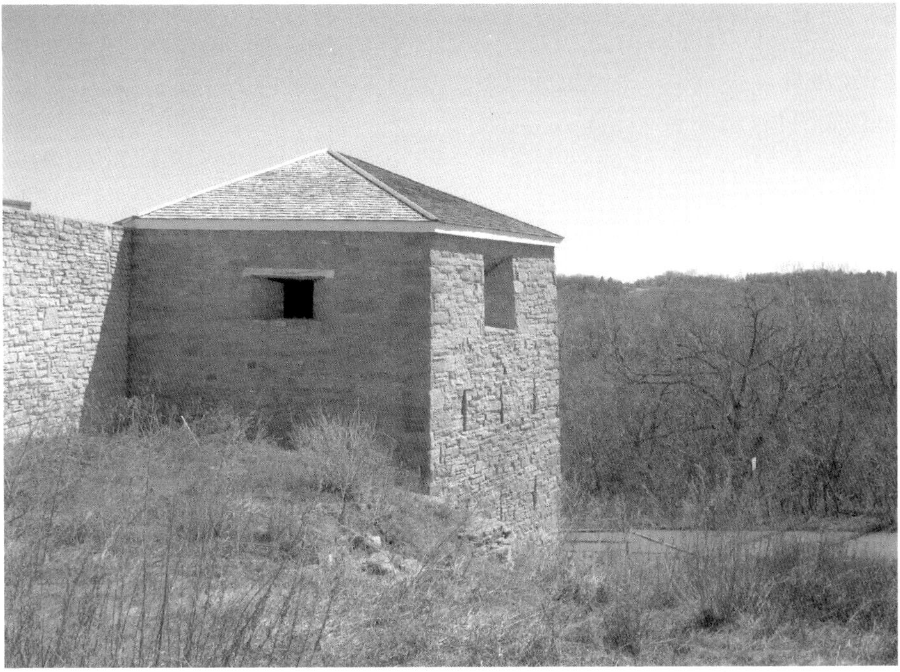

Five-sided tower at Fort Snelling, located on the confluence of the Minnesota and Mississippi Rivers in Minneapolis, Minnesota.

in the years to come will be esteemed rich mines for the historian. Early commenced, easily accomplished."

The Minnesota Historical Society was created before Minnesota even became a state, and it has one of the most significant art collections and archives in the country. It shares a judiciously edited record of events, commencing with the influx of American adventurers, U.S. military, European pioneers and missionaries. The society presents the evolution of those indigenous to the state with prudent documentation at its historic sites.

Consider the quote by George Orwell: "He who controls the past commands the future. He who commands the future conquers the past." In a struggle to understand one another and where we stand, it is helpful to have a complete and accurate record.

In the years I was growing up, I completely missed the importance of the land Fort Snelling sits on in regard to the indigenous people. I missed that the location of the fort represents the birth of the state of Minnesota. But it is much more than that. Native Americans met at the sacred junction of the

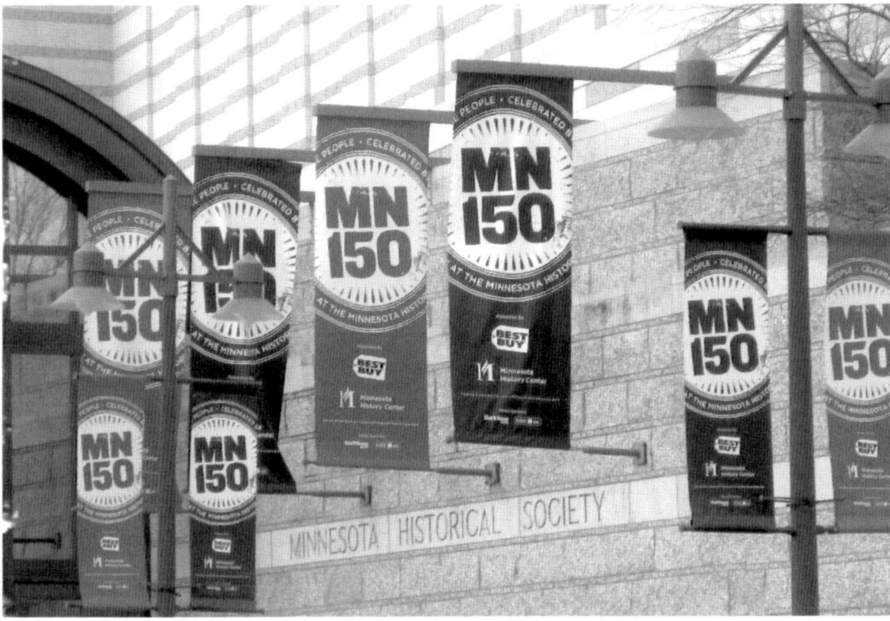

The Minnesota Historical Society in St. Paul, Minnesota.

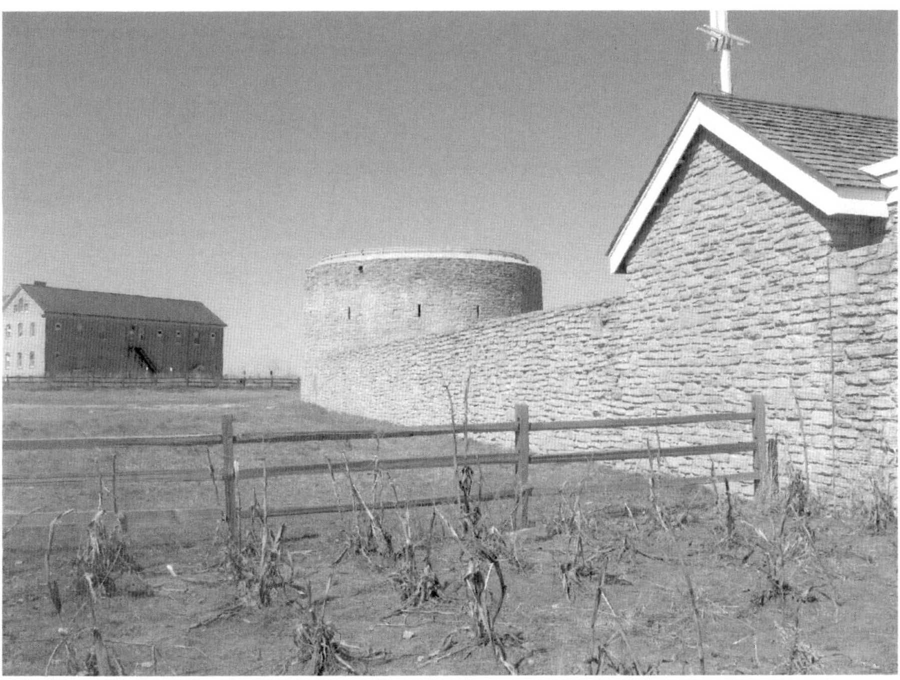

Round tower at Fort Snelling, Minneapolis, Minnesota.

Minnesota and Mississippi Rivers for thousands of years before Europeans settled here and altered the value of the river from a place of spirituality to an instrument of commerce.

A nine-thousand-year-old, five-inch-long flint spear point, used to kill mammoths twice the size of today's buffalo, was found here. It is believed to have been mined from limestone along the Minnesota River near Mankato, seventy miles to the south. That's a whole lot of history before Zebulon Pike arrived.

SACRED GROUND

The land Fort Snelling occupies represents both the beginning and the end of the Dakota. The fort was built on sacred land referred to as *Mdote* or *Bdote Minisota* by the natives. The Dakota consider this spot, where the Minnesota and Mississippi Rivers meet, their birthplace. They believe it is the center of the earth and the center of the heavens above. It is where the world began.

Dakota folklore includes a family of water spirits called the *Unktehi*, who reside in the river and are similar to Greece's god of water, Poseidon, or Italy's

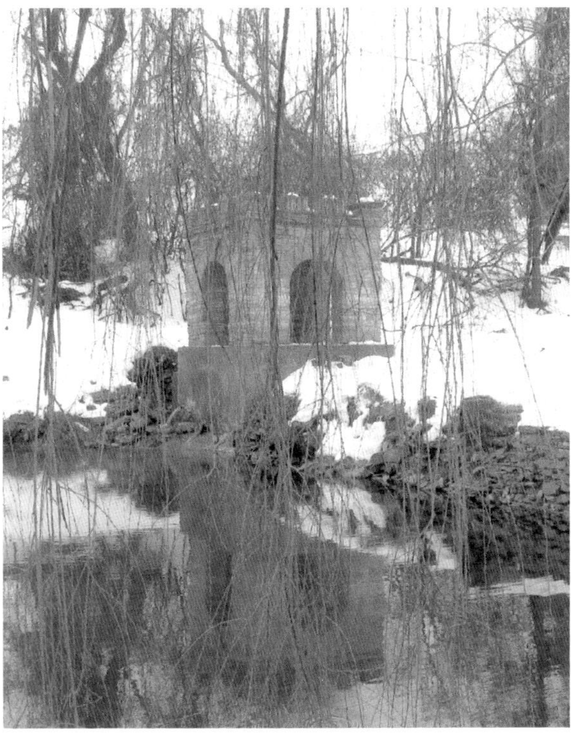

Stone arch marking the Sacred Spring near Fort Snelling, Minnesota.

sea-abiding Neptune. Dakota folklore holds that the male *Unktehi* reside in the water, and the females reside on land. The male *Unktehi* is referred to as Grandfather and the female as Grandmother. They are also referred to as *Taku-wakan*, or that which is sacred.

There are tales as far upstream the Minnesota River as Montevideo in western Minnesota about the appearance of malevolent wood sprites and other mysterious happenings, reported by campers who overnight in the heavily wooded areas alongside the river.

Unktehi are found in the water where it bubbles or in turbulent waters such as St. Anthony Falls, northeast of downtown Minneapolis. These are breathing places of the *wakan*.

Sacred Spring

For thousands of years, indigenous people have gathered for celebrations and sacred ceremonies at the sacred site, given the name Camp Coldwater by the U.S. military in the early 1800s. Water from a forty-seven-degree,

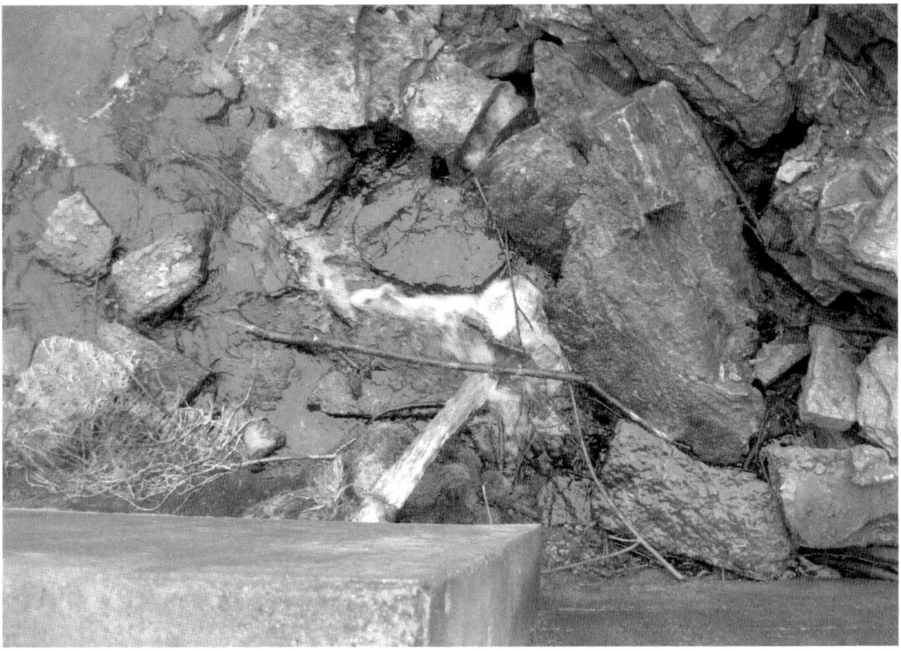

The sacred spring on the property of the abandoned Bureau of Mines campus near Fort Snelling in Minneapolis, Minnesota.

year-round spring is used in the Dakota Healing Lodge because of its purity. River or lake water would never have been used because of impurities.

In 1820, during the Lewis Cass Expedition's search for the source of the Mississippi River, American geographer, geologist, ethnologist and Indian agent Henry Rowe Schoolcraft, whose wife was of Ojibwe and Scot-Irish descent, discovered a birch bark message left by the Dakota. Found near the mouth of the Sauk River between present-day St. Cloud and Minneapolis, the message invited the Ojibwe to the sacred spring.

Science may support the healing properties of the water and the hallowed atmosphere where the two rivers meet. When solar and lunar influences cause the water table to rise, they force air, charged with negative ions, out of the earth. Negative ions are also created when the surface tension of water is broken, charging the atmosphere in much the same way a lightning strike does. Mystics have traditionally occupied waterfalls and rivers for this reason. Negative ions are associated with a sense of well-being. They lessen infections and dry burns faster, healing them more quickly and leaving less scarring.

In short, the spring water from the center of the earth is blessed.

PIKE'S PURCHASE

On September 23, 1805, New Jersey–born Lieutenant Zebulon M. Pike, for whom Pike's Peak is named, negotiated a treaty with Le Petit Carbeau and Way Aga Enogee for the land where the Minnesota and Mississippi Rivers meet.

Pike was known as a slim, blue-eyed, pompous young man with bad luck and a poor sense of direction. He is remembered for his ambition and efficiency and an odd habit of tilting his head to one side so the brim of his hat touched his shoulder. Although he attempted to, he never reached the summit of Pike's Peak, the mountain in Colorado named after him.

He was sent by the unsavory James Wilkinson, governor of the Louisiana Territory, to find the source of the Mississippi River, which Pike incorrectly identified as Leech Lake rather than Lake Itasca. A former aide to Benedict Arnold, Wilkinson was a double agent for the Spanish government. He was suspected of participating in a number of questionable activities, including the "Conway Cabal," a conspiracy to overthrow George Washington.

Wilkinson assigned his protégé, Pike, to secure land from the Indians on which to build future forts and to determine the extent of British fur trade on American soil, thereby estimating the loss in unpaid U.S. government tariffs.

Pike told the Dakota along the Minnesota River, then known as the St. Peter, that the future fort would improve their communication with the white man. He explained that this larger trading post would provide lower-priced products than those available from British fur traders. Further, he told the Native Americans that they would always be allowed to use the land.

> *Treaty with the Sioux*
> *September 23, 1805*
> *Ratified April 16, 1808.*
> *Never proclaimed by the President.*
> *Conference Between the United States of America and the Sioux Nation of Indians.*
> *Whereas, a conference held between the United States of America and the Sioux Nation of Indians, Lieut. Z.M. Pike, of the Army of the United States, and the chiefs and warriors of the said tribe, have agreed to the following articles, which when ratified and approved of by the proper authority, shall be binding on both parties:*
> *Article 1. That the Sioux Nation grants unto the United States for the purpose of the establishment of military posts, nine miles square at the mouth of the river St. Croix, also from below the confluence of the Mississippi and St. Peters, up the Mississippi, to include the falls of St. Anthony, extending nine miles on each side of the river. That the Sioux*

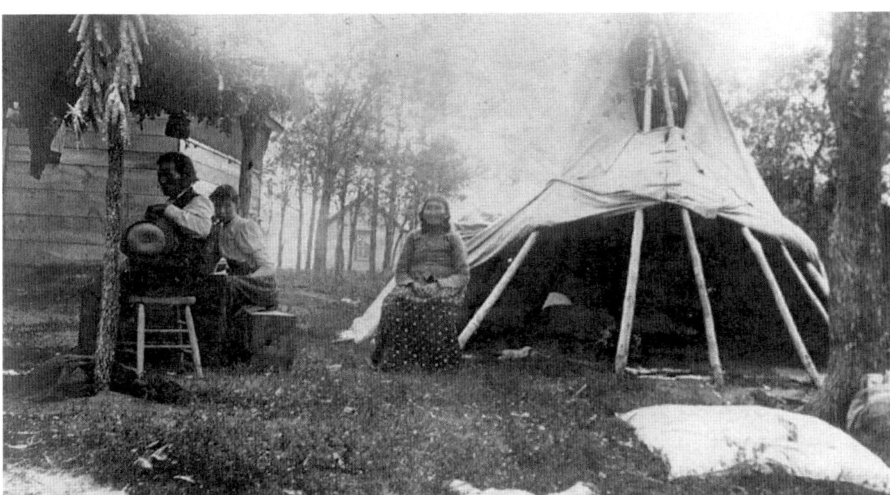

Dakota woman in front of her tipi. *Courtesy of Gary Revier, Redwood Falls, Minnesota.*

Nation grants to the United States, the full sovereignty and power over said districts forever, without any let or hindrance whatsoever.
Article 2. That in consideration of the above grants the United States (shall, prior to taking possession thereof, pay to the Sioux two thousand dollars, or deliver the value thereof in such goods and merchandise as they shall choose).
Article 3. The United States promise on their part to permit the Sioux to pass, repass, hunt or make other uses of the said districts, as they have formerly done, without any other exception, but those specified in article first.
In testimony hereof, we, the undersigned, have hereunto set our hands and seals, at the mouth of the river St. Peters, on the 23rd day of September, one thousand eight hundred and five.
Z.M. Pike, [SEAL.]
First Lieutenant and Agent at the above conference.
Le Petit Carbeau, his x mark. [SEAL.]
Way Aga Enogee, his x mark. [SEAL.]

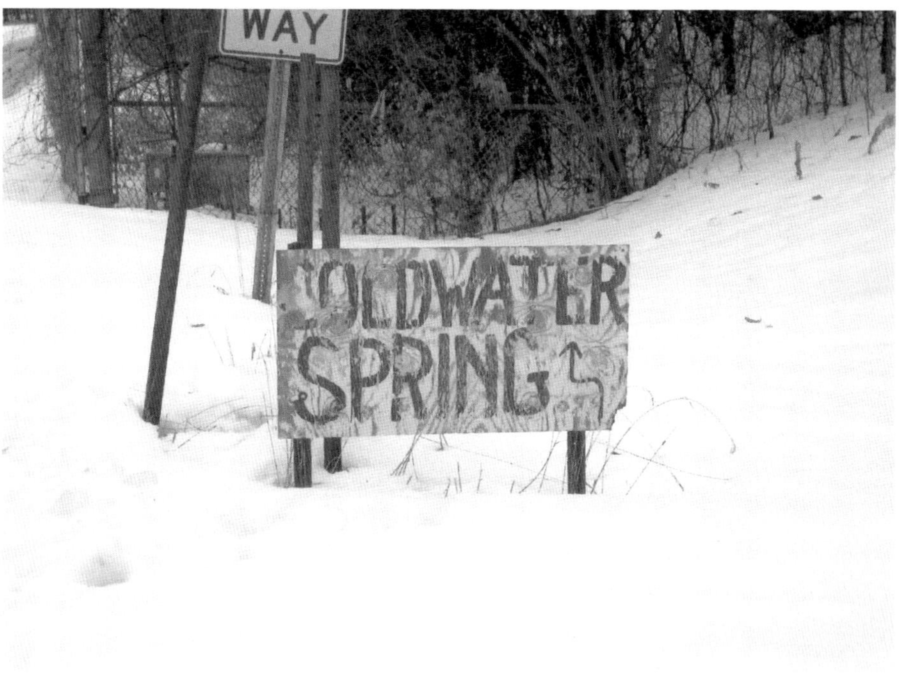

Hand-painted sign for the sacred spring, named Coldwater Spring by Colonel Leavenworth, at the entrance of the abandoned Minnesota Bureau of Mines campus near Fort Snelling, Minnesota.

Lieutenant Colonel Henry Leavenworth Leaves His Mark

In 1819, after Pike secured the agreement from the Dakota, Lieutenant Colonel Henry Leavenworth—a soldier from Connecticut and a veteran of the War of 1812—arrived in Minnesota. He led the Fifth Regiment of Infantry on construction of Fort Cantonment New Hope, along the backwaters of the Minnesota River below Mendota.

It was a difficult time for Leavenworth's troops. The soldiers found their living conditions untenable due to poor sanitary conditions and spoiled food, and the infantry experienced a 20 percent mortality rate that first year. Leavenworth moved his soldiers and their families on May 5, 1820, to the site of the sacred spring, and the area became known as Camp Coldwater. Responsibility for the location and construction of the fort was turned over to Colonel Josiah Snelling. At the sacred spring, soldiers and their families found reprieve. They raised their tents and built elm bark huts, occupying the area for three summers while they constructed the permanent fort.

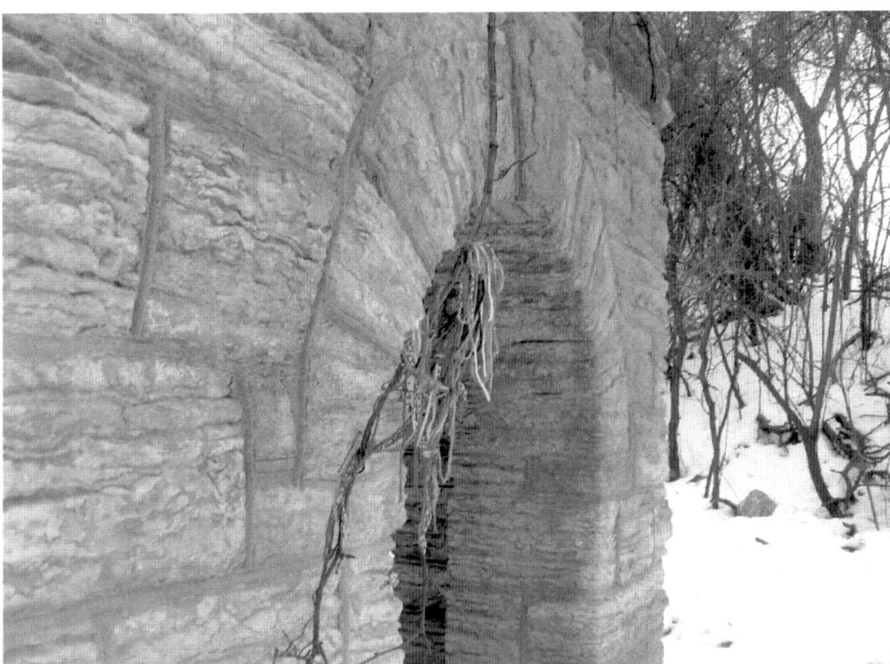

An offering left by a Native American at the stone arch at the Sacred Spring near Fort Snelling in Minneapolis, Minnesota.

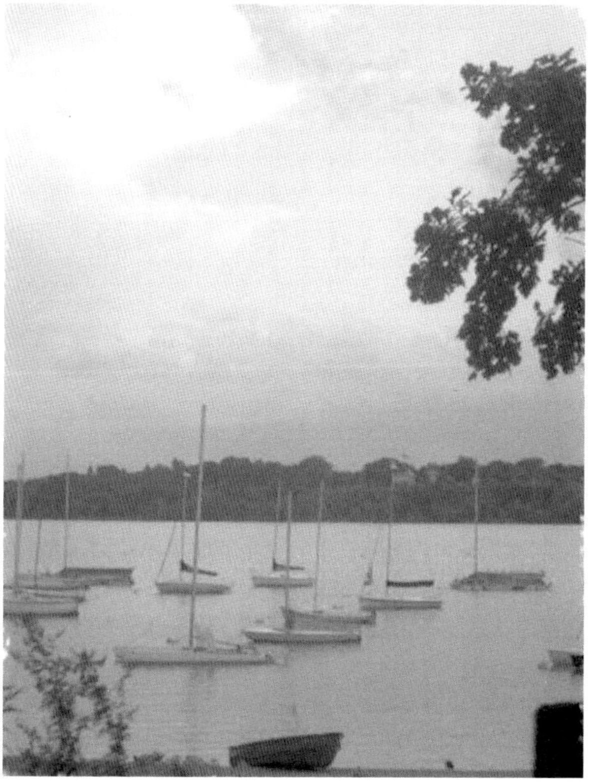

Lake Harriet in south Minneapolis, Minnesota.

A small settlement of French, Swiss, African American, Canadian, Irish and English pioneers grew up around the spring after it was vacated by the military.

Upon completion of Fort Snelling, Leavenworth went west to fight Indians. He died in 1834 while hunting buffalo. We will remember his name, however, as it has been commemorated by a variety of institutions and communities across the country, including Leavenworth, Kansas, and Leavenworth Penitentiary.

He didn't neglect to leave a mark on Minnesota. We now have within our state the community of Leavenworth in southern Minnesota. Leavenworth named Lake Harriet in south Minneapolis after his third wife, Harriet Lovejoy.

Leavenworth was initially buried in his hometown of Delhi, New York, but that didn't last long. His body was later exhumed and he was interred in—you guessed it—the Fort Leavenworth National Cemetery.

Josiah Snelling

Josiah Snelling was born and raised in Boston, Massachusetts, the son of a prominent banker. He married Elizabeth Bell, who gave birth to their son, William Joseph Snelling, in 1804. When Elizabeth died in 1810, Snelling left his six-year-old son with family members and joined the military, serving in the Battle of Tippecanoe and the War of 1812.

Snelling relieved Leavenworth of his duties in August 1820 and took over as commander of the fort until 1827. He is credited with the location, design and construction of Fort Snelling.

Pig's Eye Landing

Under the protection of the fort, squatters began taking root, among them Pierre "Pig's Eye" Parrant, a bootlegger of French-Canadian origin. Parrant was given this unflattering moniker due to blindness in one eye.

Parrant was unappreciated by the military and forced to move his operation from near the fort to a new location. He reluctantly moved five miles downstream on the north side of the river and unwittingly established the foundation of the second-largest city in Minnesota, which eventually became known as St. Paul. An additional treaty with the local tribes, signed in 1837, freed up the land for development, and by 1840 it had become a stopover for travelers moving west. As time passed, the settlement grew into a significant trade center known as Pig's Eye Landing.

When the Minnesota Territory was designated in 1849, Pig's Eye was named its capital. The community grew and eventually changed its name from Pig's Eye to St. Paul. In 1854, St. Paul became incorporated as a city.

Within a few years, over one thousand steamboats unloaded cargo and passengers annually, and eventually railroads were built to move them across the country.

The need for a fort waned, so when the military abandoned Fort Snelling, the government put it up for sale. The fort was next used primarily as a pen for sheep. On June 8, 1857, a year before Minnesota became a state, Franklin Steele purchased the old fort for $90,000. A brother-in-law of Henry Hastings Sibley, the first governor of Minnesota, Steele had been a storekeeper at the fort and planned to plat the land for a new community.

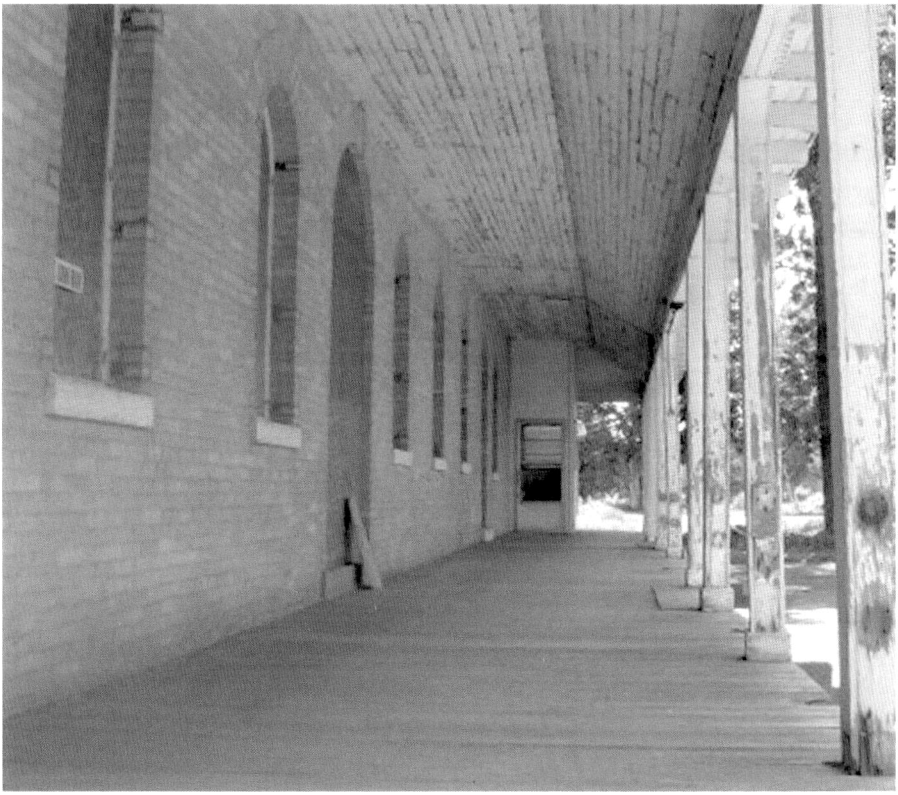

Abandoned building at Fort Snelling in Minneapolis, Minnesota.

Plans to create a city on the Fort Snelling property were, however, suddenly altered in 1860 at the outset of the Civil War. Once again, Fort Snelling was employed with the training of volunteers for the Union army.

Dred Scott's Fort Snelling Days Help Spark the Civil War

Dred Scott was brought to Fort Snelling while it was still part of the Wisconsin Territory in the 1830s by his master, Dr. John Emerson, a military surgeon. Emerson purchased Scott from the Peter Blow family in Missouri. The Blows had moved from the state of Alabama to the newly acquired Louisiana Territory but had not prospered as hoped. As a result of financial pressure after the death of her spouse, Mrs. Blow was forced to sell assets, one of which was Scott.

While residing with his master at Fort Snelling, Scott met Harriet Robinson, a woman born into slavery in the state of Virginia in 1815. Robinson was owned by Major Lawrence Taliaferro, a federal Indian agent assigned in the early 1820s from Virginia to Fort Snelling, where he served for almost twenty years. He had a reputation as a gentleman who supported the rights of Native Americans.

Although slaves continued to travel with their owners in free states, serving as valets and maids, slavery was not allowed at Fort Snelling. This was due to the Missouri Compromise, an agreement struck by Congress in 1820 between members who supported slavery and those who didn't. The northern and western regions of the country were antislavery, while the older states to the south and east, whose economy was based on the premise of slave labor, were proslavery. The compromise excluded slavery from the Missouri Territory north of the parallel 36°30' north (the southern boundary of Missouri), except within the limits of the proposed state of Missouri. The angry and emotional debate about slavery between the members of Congress was a sign of the danger that lay ahead for a Union deeply divided by moral and economic differences.

Scott and Robinson met at Fort Snelling and were married in a civil ceremony by Taliaferro. Emerson was transferred to Fort Jesup in Louisiana, and he asked the Scotts to join him. Emerson died in 1843, and his wife became owner of the couple.

In the spring of 1846, while living in proslavery St. Louis, Harriet and Dred each filed a suit for their freedom, based on having lived as free individuals at Fort Snelling and other free territories.

Their first case was dismissed on a technicality, due to hearsay admitted as evidence. But on January 12, 1850, the Scotts were granted a short-lived freedom. During the legal proceedings, they were supported by sons of Scott's first master, the Blows, who had grown up with him.

After her husband's death, Irene Emerson moved in with her proslavery father, Alexander Sanford, on his plantation in north St. Louis County, Missouri. For the next three years, Harriet and Dred worked for other people while Mrs. Emerson collected their wages.

Her brother, John F.A. Sanford, did not like the decision, which had an economic impact on them. Mrs. Emerson and her brother filed a suit against the Scotts, the explosive *Dred Scott v. Irene Emerson* case, and the court decision to allow the Scotts their freedom was reversed.

On March 6, 1857, seven of the nine justices agreed that Dred and Harriet Scott should remain slaves. It was also determined that as slaves, the

Scotts were not citizens of the United States and therefore had no right to bring suit in the federal courts on any matter. In addition, the court declared that the Scotts had never been free, due to the fact that slaves were personal property; thus, the Missouri Compromise of 1820 was unconstitutional, and the federal government had no right to prohibit slavery in the new territories.

If it hadn't been for the death of Mrs. Emerson's brother and her remarriage to an antislavery congressman, Calvin Chafee, the Scotts might never have won their freedom. As it stood, Chafee insisted that his wife transfer ownership of the Scotts back to Taylor Blow, son of Dred Scott's first master. Blow granted them their freedom in 1857. Dred Scott lived as a free man for only one year before he died of tuberculosis.

Concentration Camp on Pike's Island

In the summer of 1862, just a few years after treaties had been negotiated by Alexander Ramsey, who eventually became the second governor of Minnesota, seven thousand Dakota people were starving on a small parcel of land along the Minnesota River Valley. Unscrupulous fur traders had schemed to collect the annuities promised in treaties to the Native Americans, claiming that the tribes owed them money for purchases made at the trading posts. The Indians watched as land they had previously been free to travel over and provide for their families on became occupied by a foreign nation.

In the process of forcing the tribe onto a reservation, the Dakota were also forced to adopt European ways in dress, language and livelihood. They were mandated to raise crops and livestock on a small bit of land that was much better suited for hunting and fishing. There had been a potato blight, and they were starving.

The Dakota knew the warehouse was full of food, seeds and items required to sustain them, but they were denied access. The annuity payment, which was to be delivered to them by boat on the Minnesota River, grew later and later as the American government debated whether to pay in gold or paper. The Civil War was draining their coffers, and in the meantime, the Dakota suffered.

On August 15, 1862, a small group of Indians, led by Chief Little Crow, was summoned by Indian agent Thomas Galbraith to join him and trader Andrew Myrick at the Lower Sioux Agency to discuss the state of affairs. Galbraith had at his disposition the ability to release the supplies from the stone warehouse, and he had done so in tiny portions. But being a stickler

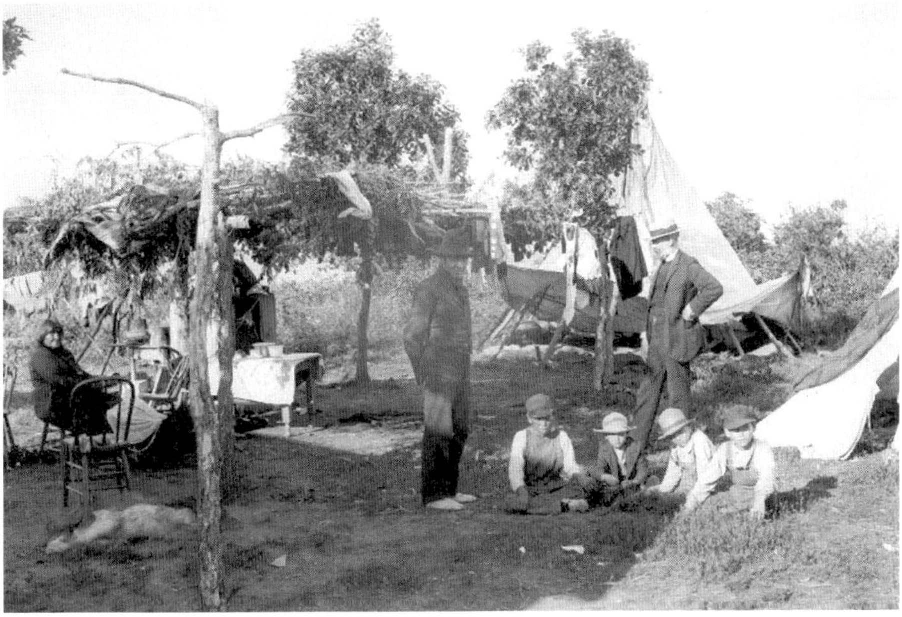

Dakota family after the conflict of 1862. *Courtesy of Gary Revier, Redwood Falls, Minnesota.*

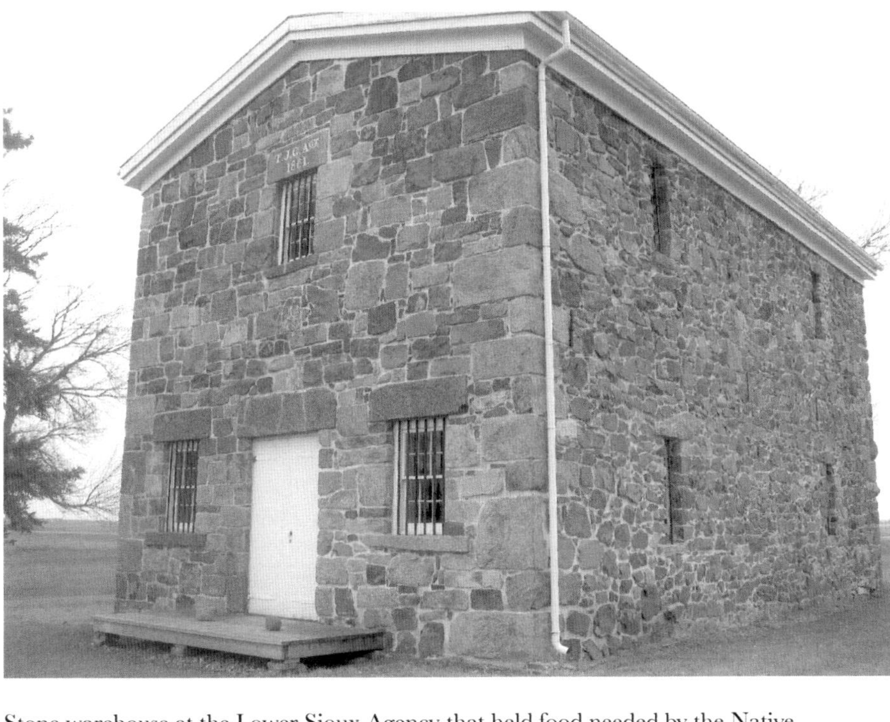

Stone warehouse at the Lower Sioux Agency that held food needed by the Native Americans in 1862.

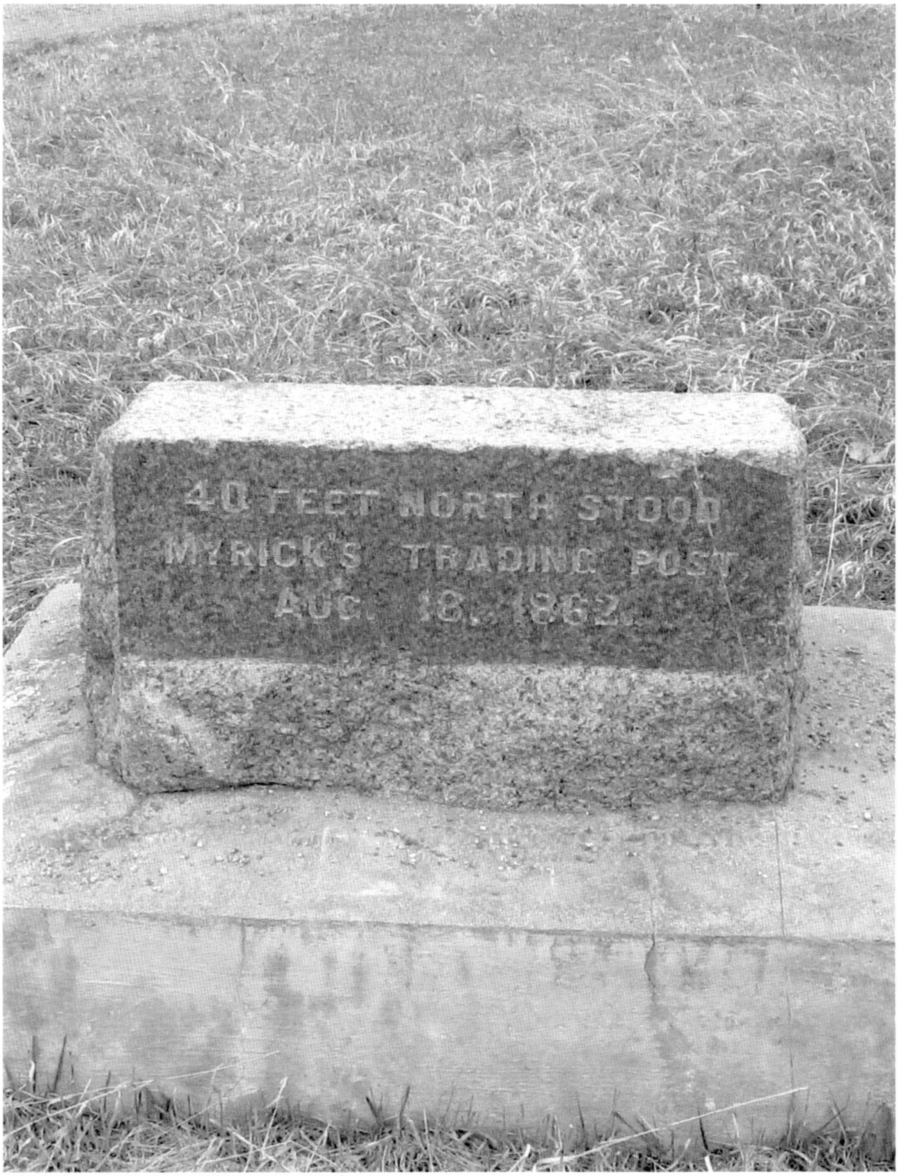

Stone marking Myrick's trading post at the Lower Sioux reservation near Morton, Minnesota.

for details, he refused to open the doors to the tribe on the grounds that the annuity payments and the release of warehouse goods must be undertaken at the same time.

The tribe members complained to the men that the white man was hunting on their land, felling trees for timber and cutting grass for livestock. They told Myrick and Galbraith to keep the settlers off their land. In one of the most pivotal moments in the history of the Minnesota River Valley and in American history, Myrick declared, "So far as I am concerned, if they are hungry, let them eat grass or their own dung!" The statement was followed by complete silence.

On August 18, Myrick was found dead outside his trading post, his mouth stuffed with grass. The U.S. Dakota Conflict of 1862 had begun.

Within months, the Dakota had been defeated by the American government, and Governor Alexander Ramsey declared that Native Americans must be extinguished. The surviving 1,700 Dakota surrendered to Colonel Henry Sibley at Camp Release along the western end of the Minnesota River Valley near Montevideo, where they released 269 white captives.

The Dakota were taken prisoner, their ranks made up mostly of women, children and elders. The survivors were driven over one hundred miles east to the Pike's Island internment camp at Fort Snelling. The prisoners were abused by the white settlers as they were marched through river valley communities.

Over three hundred Native Americans died on Pike's Island the first year from food poisoning, illness, starvation and exposure. The following is a list of the Dakota prisoners as compiled by the U.S. Army on December 2, 1862. (The number next to the name refers to how many were from that tribe or family.)

Wapahasa's Band (196)
Passing Hail's Band (227)
Red Leg's Band (172)
Wakute's Band (254)
Eagle Head's Band (130)
Black Dog's Band (74)
Good Road's Band (119)
Taopi's Band (390)
Yellow Medicine's Band (664)

Mixed Blood Families (142)
John Moore 5
Angus M. Robertson 1
Gustavus A. Robertson 1
Thomas A. Robertson 2
Jane Moore 1
Joseph E. LaFramboise 4
Louise Moore 3
Louise Frenier 2
Narcisse Frenier 3
Alexis E. LaFramboise 3
Thomas Robinson 2
Louison Frenier 8
Jack Frasier 1
Joseph Lablac 8
David Fairebault 1
Joseph Monterey 2
Mary Tussotts 1
A.D. Campbell 8
Scott Campbell 5
Antoine Renville 7
Michael Renville 6
Gabriel Renville 8
Charles Crawford 1
Frances Roy 8
Vetal Boye 3
Daniel Renville 4
Joseph Renville 2
Rosalie Renville 2
Maline Mumford 4
Alek Graham 6

Of these prisoners, 303 Dakota men were condemned to death in makeshift trials. All but 38 had their sentences commuted by President Abraham Lincoln. The 38 were hanged simultaneously from a huge scaffold on Main Street in Mankato during the largest mass execution to take place in the United States. Their bodies were buried in a shallow grave on the sandy shore of the Minnesota River but were quickly removed and sold as far east as Chicago, Illinois, for medical research.

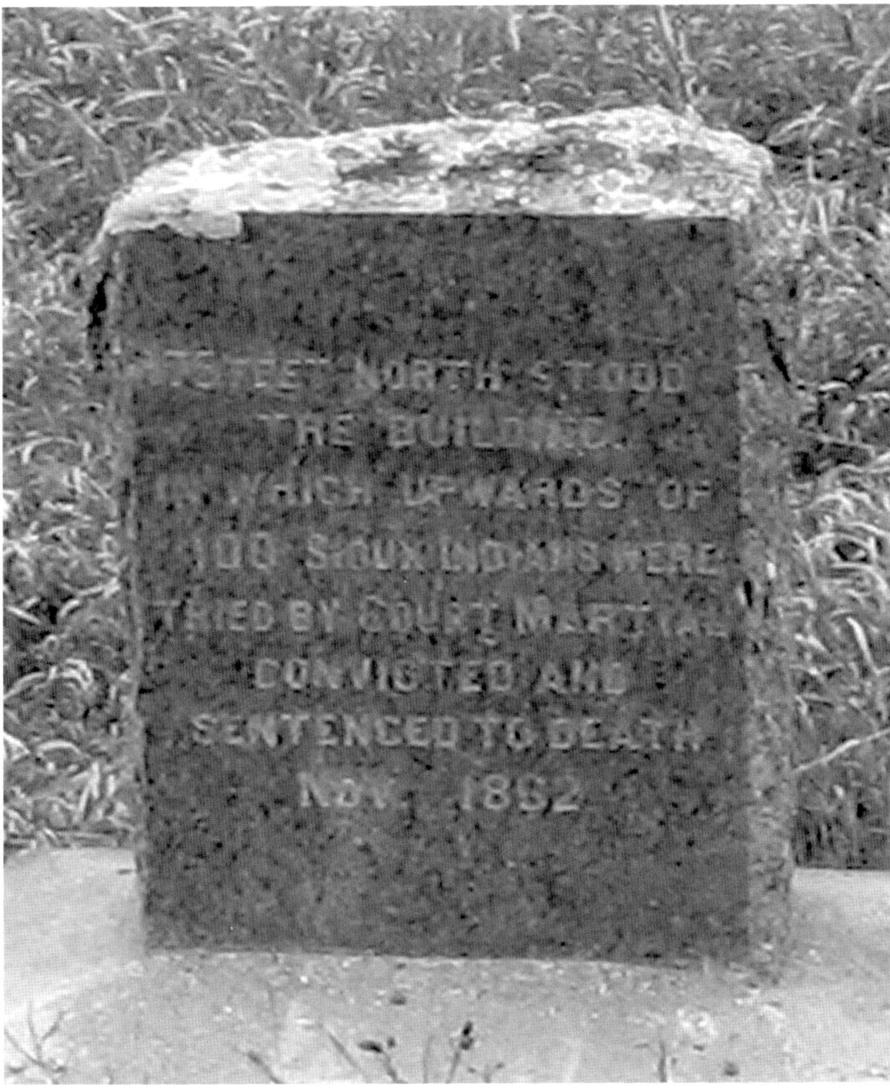

Court-martial site at the Lower Sioux Agency near Morton, Minnesota.

The surviving Pike's Island prisoners were eventually removed to other parts of the country, and a bounty was put on the heads of Native Americans remaining in Minnesota.

Fort Snelling After the Civil War

After the Civil War ended, Fort Snelling became the headquarters and supply station for the Department of Dakota, which extended from the Mississippi River to the Rocky Mountains. The regulars from Fort Snelling served in a campaign to eradicate Native Americans from the region and also served in the Spanish-American War of 1898.

At the time of Christopher Columbus's arrival in the New World, the Native American population living in what is now the United States was estimated at about one million. By 1880, only 250,000 Indians remained.

By the time World War II rolled around in 1939, the population had risen to about 350,000. Fort Snelling processed over 300,000 inductees during the Second World War, 44,000 of whom were Native Americans. During World War II, Fort Snelling once again served as an internment camp, this time for Japanese Americans.

The end of World War II also marked the decline of Fort Snelling. Its buildings were shared by other organizations like the Veterans Administration and the Bureau of Mines.

In 1950, a highway was proposed to run through the fort. This brought the structure to the public's attention, and the general consensus favored

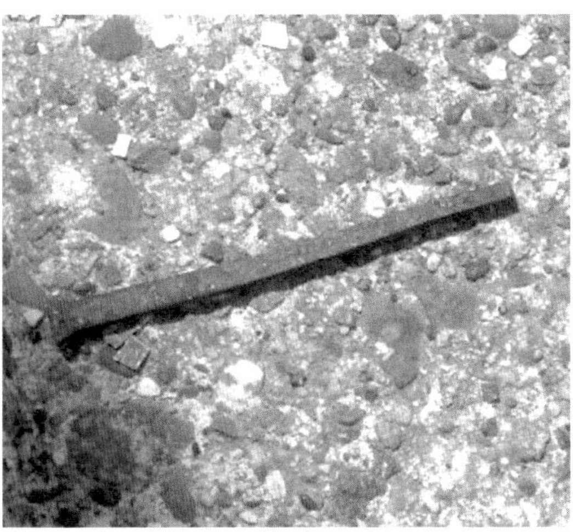

Square nail from a rundown building at Fort Snelling in Minneapolis, Minnesota.

saving the fort through designation as a National Historic Landmark. The fort was awarded the designation in 1960.

Minnesota Mystery

Dear Diary,

After I read about the sacred spring at Camp Coldwater I had to see it for myself, so Melanie picked me up and we headed out. We met a nice police officer at the entry to the sacred spring who told us the spring was at the end of the road. We had to park our car and go in by foot.

We hiked through the old abandoned Bureau of Mines Campus, occasionally slipping on the ice, and almost gave up on finding the spring until we saw the arches built of stone, marking the spring.

We looked at the offerings left by visiting Native Americans, then held hands and prayed for their future. Call me a conspiracy theorist—but my overly active imagination thinks there is more here than meets the eye.

"Article 3. The United States promise on their part to permit the Sioux to pass, repass, hunt or make other uses of the said districts, as they have formerly done, without any other exception, but those specified in article first."

An Environmental Impact Study (EIS) was done on the Camp Coldwater acreage after the closing of the Minnesota Bureau of Mines, to determine future use of the land. The Dakota tribes are asking for the land to be returned to them as a sacred spot to resume their ceremonies and celebrations without having to get governmental permission.

The survey was based on the premise that the area was first occupied by Leavenworth's regiment and says little of the use of the land by the Dakota previous to that.

The EIS was used by the National Park Service to consider granting this request. After further study, the National Park Service's analysis and report concludes:

"There is the danger that we would be giving a site a meaning and power for the Dakota that it did not historically have. If the evidence does not support historical use of the spring by the Dakota for any day to day or special ceremonial use, then maybe it was not special to them. If this were the case, then we (and all those non-Dakota interests who support giving the spring a special designation) may be creating Dakota history, rather than recording it. Since this process will be well documented, what we say now about Coldwater Spring will become permanent fact." Um, really? It's a head-scratcher. So, here's what I want to know…

1. Why did the federal government build the Minnesota Bureau of Mines on the thirty acres considered sacred and a meeting place of the Dakota for thousands of years, and was also of historical significance regarding the salvation of the military families who were dying on the Minnesota River backwaters?

2. In a state where our historical society is older than Minnesota itself, why hasn't the site been well marked, interpreted and promoted like the battle sites commemorating the U.S. Dakota Conflict of 1862?

3. Why have the Dakota been denied free access to the site for almost two hundred years when the treaty of 1805 said they would have it?

4. When the Bureau of Mines built its campus, why were nine feet of soil laid upon the existing land before construction?

5. When the contract for the Environmental Impact Study was drawn up, why was it based on the following premise—the area designated as Camp Coldwater was an area first occupied by Anglo-Americans from 1820 to 1823 by the Fifth Infantry under the command of Lieutenant

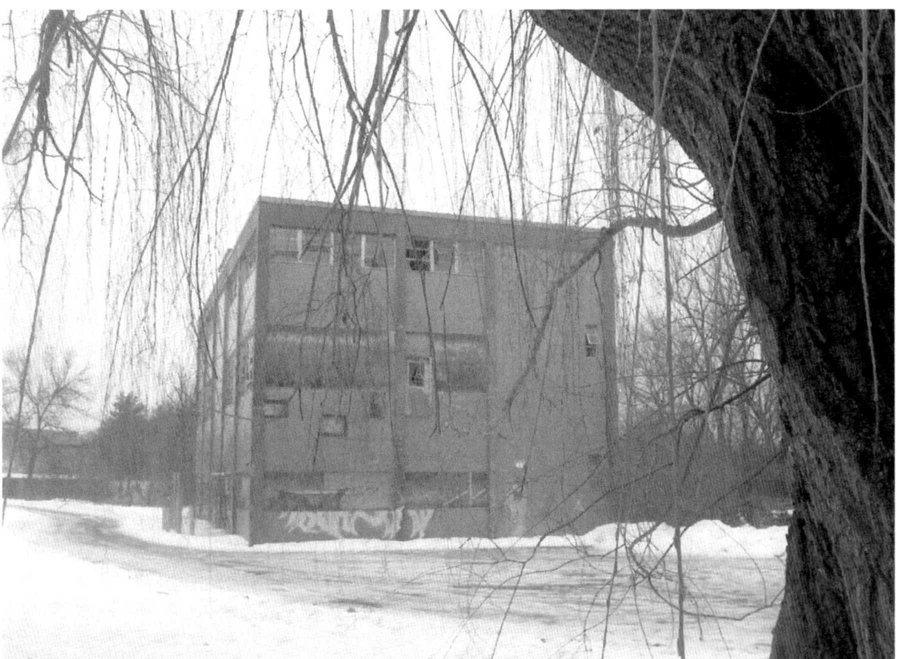

Abandoned building at the Minnesota Bureau of Mines campus near Fort Snelling in Minneapolis, Minnesota.

Colonel Henry Leavenworth—and fail to mention its use by the pre-Columbian Dakota for so many centuries prior?

6. Why is the federal government opposed to returning a mere thirty acres to the tribes who still leave offerings at the sacred spring and pray there?

7. Does the group studying the EIS have a Native American as a member? I'm just asking.

—Minnesota Country Mouse

Native American Dispute with the U.S. Bureau of Mines

On May 16, 1910, Congress passed the Organic Act (Public Law 179) establishing the agency known as the U.S. Bureau of Mines (USBM). In the late 1950s, the Veterans Association transferred forty-three acres, including the sacred spring, to the Department of the Interior, and the Minneapolis Bureau of Mines campus was constructed.

From 1960 until 1995, the Mining Center produced mine safety equipment, developed solutions for safer mining worldwide and studied economic conditions affecting the industry. After the closure of the Minnesota Bureau of Mines, the Dakota found themselves in a battle with the U.S. government for the right to reclaim the sacred spring and surrounding land for tribal ceremonies. The circumstances surrounding the federal government's hesitation are a bit of a modern mystery.

Fort Snelling is now a historic site open to the public with tours and an interpretive center.

Alexander Ramsey Park

Baby Goats

Dear Diary,

I was just looking at the KLGR AM Radio website, out of Redwood Falls in southwestern Minnesota, this morning, and I see the Alexander Ramsey Park zoo has some new baby bison and deer.

Heck, it's worth taking a drive through that huge, beautiful park just to feed your soul—even if you skipped the zoo. (Though, who would want to do that?)

I wonder if there are any new baby goats. You can stick a quarter in a little machine near their pen, then turn the crank and feed them kernels of corn. This is a strategy I would recommend, because corn makes you very popular with goats.

—Minnesota Country Mouse

I was blessed with parents who completely appreciate their home on the southwestern Minnesota prairie. On Sunday afternoons, my folks, and whoever wanted to ride along, would pile into the old green station wagon for a close-to-home adventure. We'd explore the Minnesota River Valley, sometimes visiting Alexander Ramsey Park and zoo in Redwood Falls. In that case, we'd top off our day with a picnic of hot dogs, toasted marshmallows and cold A&W root beer served from a sweating amber jug.

Those were sweet times.

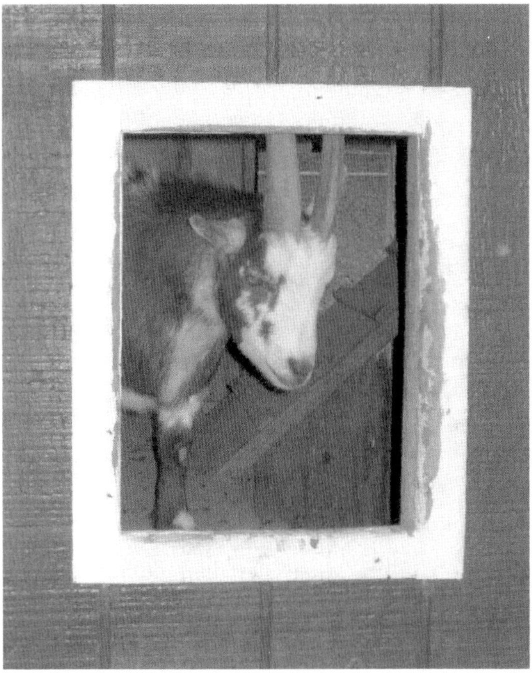

Goat at the Alexander Ramsey Park zoo.

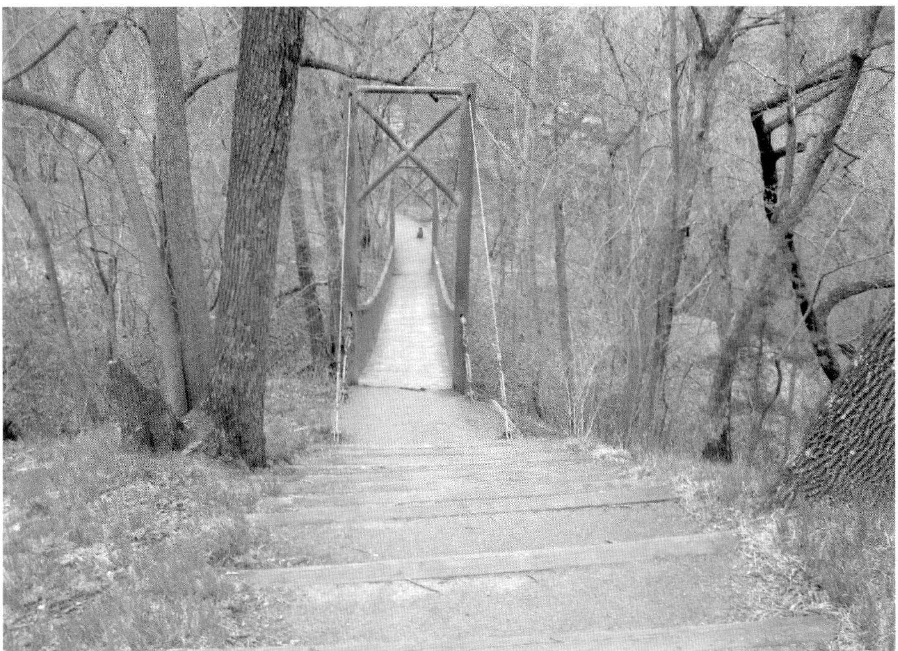

Suspended bridge leading to the falls in Alexander Ramsey Park, Redwood Falls, Minnesota. *Courtesy of Gary Revier, Redwood Falls, Minnesota.*

With ballparks, campgrounds, bison, scenic outlooks and a DNR trout stream, 216-acre Alexander Ramsey Park kept us kids busy. But it was the architecture in this largest of Minnesota's municipal parks that warmed my heart. Sturdy granite structures, the result of public works projects implemented during the Depression, brought relief to the unemployed during the 1930s. Today those structures—granite restrooms, a bridge and the lower shelter, magnificently constructed with massive timbers—still serve park visitors. It is the granite swaybacked bridge crossing the Redwood River that I find most magnificent.

The state history of this picturesque park stretches back to 1911, when the State of Minnesota purchased this mostly wooded ravine for public use. Ramsey Creek runs through the park, pouring over a granite ledge in a substantial fifty-foot waterfall, and meets up with the Redwood River. In 1957, the state turned the park over to the City of Redwood Falls.

It is as though God, in creating this scenic area, pressed his thumb smartly into the otherwise flat prairie landscape, giving flatlanders a break from the stark, ever-present, 360-degree horizon line.

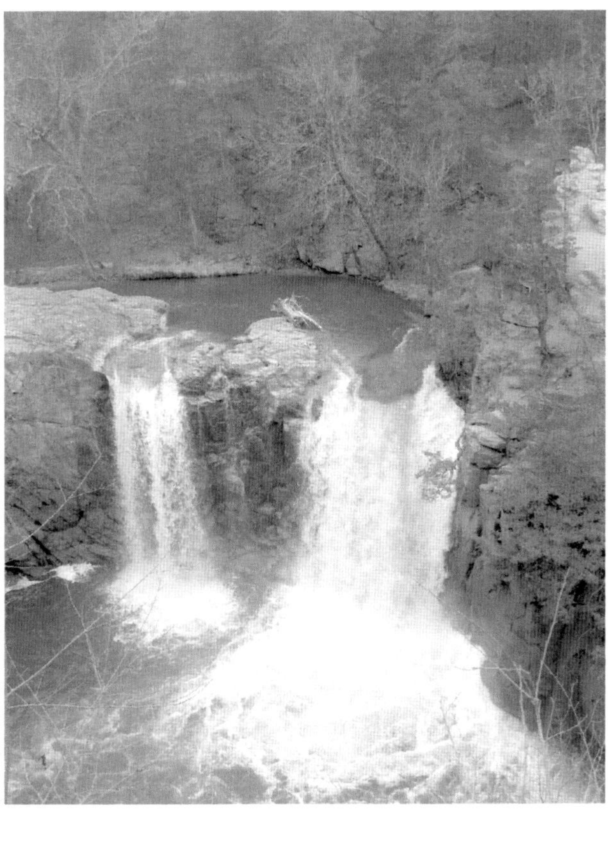

Ramsey Falls in Alexander Ramsey Park, Redwood Falls, Minnesota.

Riding through the park as a child, I stared through the windows of the old station wagon, eyes wide open, terrified by the hairpin curves and steep ravines along the narrow, winding road. And although I have never once heard of such a thing happening in Ramsey Park, I was certain we would plummet over the edge to our untimely deaths. The road has since been paved and widened, but the ride is still thrilling.

The Naming of Redwood Falls

I was curious how the name Redwood Falls was given to the city that is home to Alexander Ramsey Park. Thank goodness I was told of local historian Gary Revier, who provided the following piece of information. According to Gary, the Dakota, or Sioux, lived primarily in Wisconsin and northern Minnesota. Their traditional enemies were the Ojibwa, or Chippewa. The Dakota were being driven farther south and finally arrived at the junction of the Minnesota and Mississippi Rivers.

Hunting parties ventured up the valley of the Minnesota and onto the prairies of southern Minnesota. Being nomadic, their families would follow the main hunting parties. In 1740, according to the Dakota calendar, a large party came to the Valley of Redwood and encamped in the area of the present-day Redwood Falls cemetery. It was described as a large village made up of a thousand teepees.

The Dakota sent a scouting party into the Minnesota Valley, which they followed to the junction of the Redwood River. Going up the Redwood Valley, they came to a waterfall and crossed to the west side of the river. Upon reaching that side of the river, they found a large village of northern Cheyenne. There are differences of opinion as to the Indian nation. As the scouts moved, they had painted red spots on trees and rocks to point the way for the main war party. The Dakota achieved full strength and began an attack on the Cheyenne village. The running battle continued all the way to the spirit lake in Iowa.

The Dakota were victorious in the extremely bloody war and returned to the falls of the redwood. They painted a pole, or tree, red and held a sun dance to honor the spirits and celebrate the victory. The dance was held annually for many years at a site along the river. It was described as where the river bends.

The river and village became known as *Cansayapi Otonwe*, chaw shi apay o tune way, or "where they paint the tree red," later to be known by the white settlers as Redwood. The "Falls" was added by Sam McPhail for obvious reasons. The original name the whites gave the village of Redwood Falls was Fort Hilmer.

The Naming of Alexander Ramsey Park

Gary also provided the following information regarding the dedication of Ramsey Park in 1912. Hiram Hitchcock, son of the first Redwood County medical director and founder of what is now Sward Kemp Drug, is the person who chose the name of the park. Ramsey's daughter attended the dedication on June 28, 1912. Ramsey did not travel this far west of the Lower Sioux Agency at Morton.

As a showpiece, the state located the figurehead of the decommissioned battleship USS *Minnesota* in the park. It was later stolen and melted down for the bronze, in spite of being a huge and heavy artifact.

Alexander Ramsey

I spent hours and hours playing and picnicking at the park as a child, but I'd never given the name—Alexander Ramsey—much thought. My curiosity eventually got the best of me, and I discovered a nineteenth-century urban pioneer behind the name. Ramsey, who held numerous political offices including one as Minnesota's first territorial governor, had a political reputation for moderation. Some occasionally criticized his desire to bridge the gap between opposing parties as a sign of weakness.

Ramsey was born in Hummelstown, Pennsylvania, in 1815. When Ramsey was only eleven, his father died, and he was sent to Harrisburg to live with Frederick Kelker, his mother's uncle. There he worked in a hardware store and apprenticed as a carpenter.

As an adult, Ramsey stood nearly six feet tall and weighed 190 pounds, with broad shoulders and a reputation for enjoying food and drink. When he drank, he "stood it better than most." Although considered by friends and family to be of moderate intelligence and lacking in any noticeable talent, Ramsey managed to become the secretary of a literary society, his first office. It seems he accepted others' limited views of himself, making the most of it. When making a point in a conversation or speech, Ramsey generally took the simplest and most direct route to reach it.

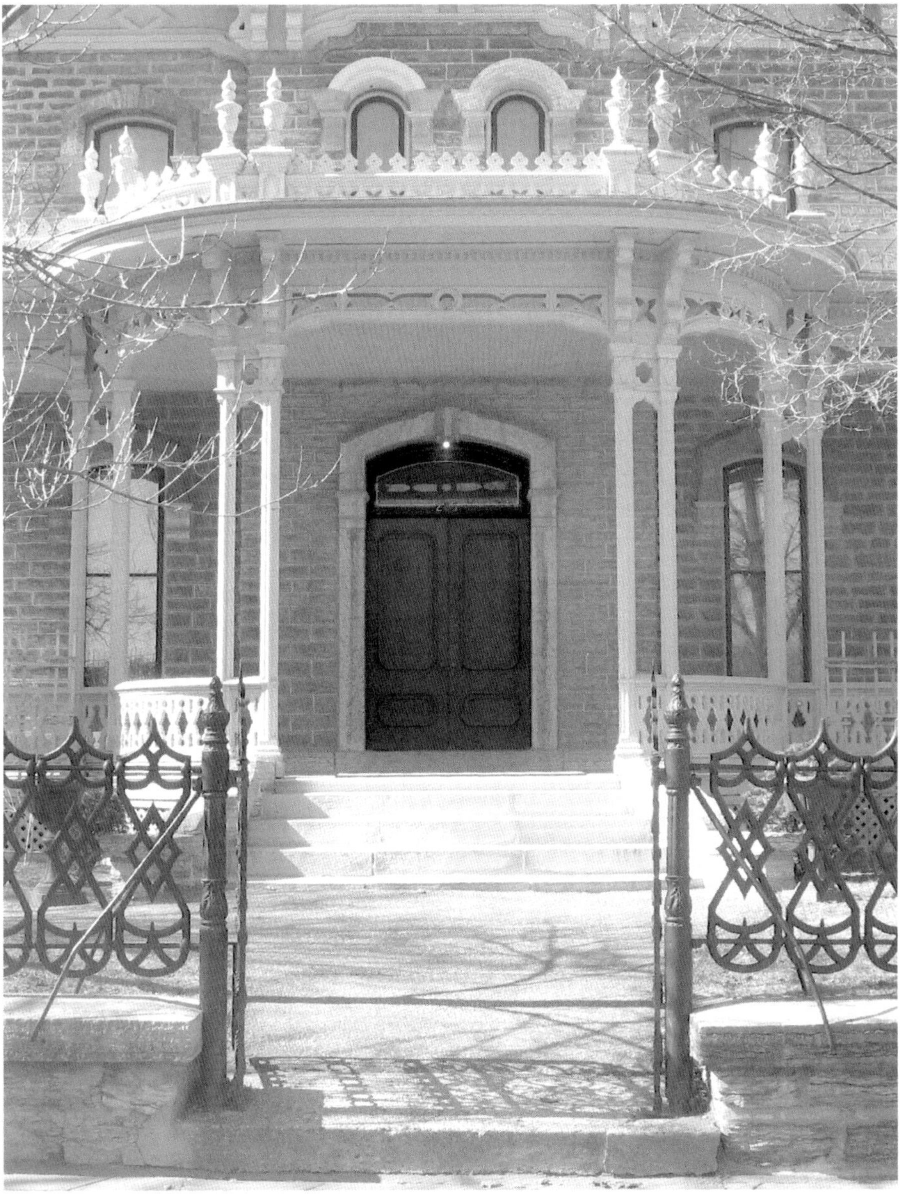

Doorway to the Alexander Ramsey House in St. Paul, Minnesota.

In 1834, he enrolled in the Manual Labor Academy of Lafayette College at Easton, Pennsylvania. He worked as a carpenter to help pay his tuition. He attended school for two terms and then became a teacher at Kutztown Franklin Academy.

Ramsey became involved in local politics, declaring, "I bid fair to be an honest politician, a race of men as rare in these days as good men in Sodom in the days of Lot." He also began writing about politics for the local newspaper, signing his contributions "Junius," a pseudonym for the prolific political writer whose contributions to the eighteenth-century London newspaper the *Public Advertiser* he admired.

Ramsey was elected from Pennsylvania to serve as a Whig in the U.S. House of Representatives from March 1843 to March 1847. During that time, in 1845, he married Anna Earl Jenks from Bucks County, Pennsylvania. Her father served in Congress. They had three children, two of whom died in childhood.

Governor of Minnesota Territory, 1849 to 1853

Ramsey's commitment to politics deepened as the country moved treacherously toward a clash of ideals between northern and southern states. The South intended to hold on to its plantation system–based economy. And there was growing concern in the South about the area's influence in government due to significant growth in the North.

Many of the growing pains suffered in the mid-1800s resulted from opposing opinions on slavery in the United States. The Ramseys had an African servant, Martha E. Clark Hall, who was a member of the household while the family resided in St. Paul and later in Washington, D.C.

On the topic of slavery, Ramsey declared, "I am neither an Abolitionist, Colonizationalist, nor yet an Amalgamationist." Still, he worked with Whigs to support "Old Rough and Ready" slave owner Zachary Taylor, from the South, in his campaign for president in 1848. In return for Ramsey's support, Taylor appointed him governor of the Minnesota Territory on April 2, 1849.

In May 1849, Ramsey, his wife and son, their servant Mrs. Hall, Ramsey's brother Justus and Ramsey's secretary, Dr. Thomas Foster, traveled by train and river steamboats to the new territory of Minnesota. There, fur trader Henry H. Sibley, a Democrat and Minnesota's delegate to Congress, greeted the Ramsey entourage. Sibley gave Ramsey his first tour of the territory, impressing upon him the importance of traders in Minnesota politics.

Ramsey's membership in the Whig Party made his transition to governor in the heavily Democratic territory of Minnesota challenging. Territorial secretary Charles K. Smith, a controversial figure frequently at odds with his colleagues, often disagreed with Ramsey's policies. Smith further inflamed the situation by inspiring a circular that accused Ramsey of being nothing more than a "Pennsylvania coffee house politician." He further accused Ramsey of "speculation" and "anti-Whig activity."

As governor, Ramsey made land-cession treaties with the Indians a primary goal of his administration. In 1851, Ramsey and Commissioner of Indian Affairs Luke Lea were appointed to negotiate treaties with Dakota tribes at Mendota and Traverse des Sioux. This was an attempt to move the tribes off land encroached upon by white settlers. The treaties were ratified in 1852 and set off a series of events leading to the eventual starvation and near extinction of Native Americans.

Governor of Minnesota, 1860 to 1863

After completing his term as territorial governor in 1853, Ramsey next served as mayor of St. Paul from 1855 to 1860. On January 2, 1860, he was elected the second governor of Minnesota. Ramsey is credited with being the first Union governor to commit troops to the American Civil War, which was due in part to his presence in Washington, D.C. He was attending the 1860 Republican National Convention in our nation's capital when the war broke out.

But back in Minnesota, Ramsey faced other issues, most notably those dealing with the growing conflict between settlers and indigenous tribes. After being herded onto small tracts of land along the Minnesota River, the native peoples were hungry. Yet they risked death if they left the reservations to hunt for food.

By the summer of 1862, Native American men had watched their wives and babies and elders become malnourished and sick, knowing the stone warehouse at the Lower Sioux Agency, near Morton, was full of food intended for them. But, because of late annuity payments and strict legal protocol, that food was left undistributed.

The Native Americans began a battle that they lost decisively. The devastating U.S.-Dakota Conflict marked a pivotal point in the Minnesota River Valley's history.

In 1863, as a result of their war against the U.S. government, Ramsey declared a $25 bounty on the scalps of the native people. He eventually paid as much as $200 for a scalp.

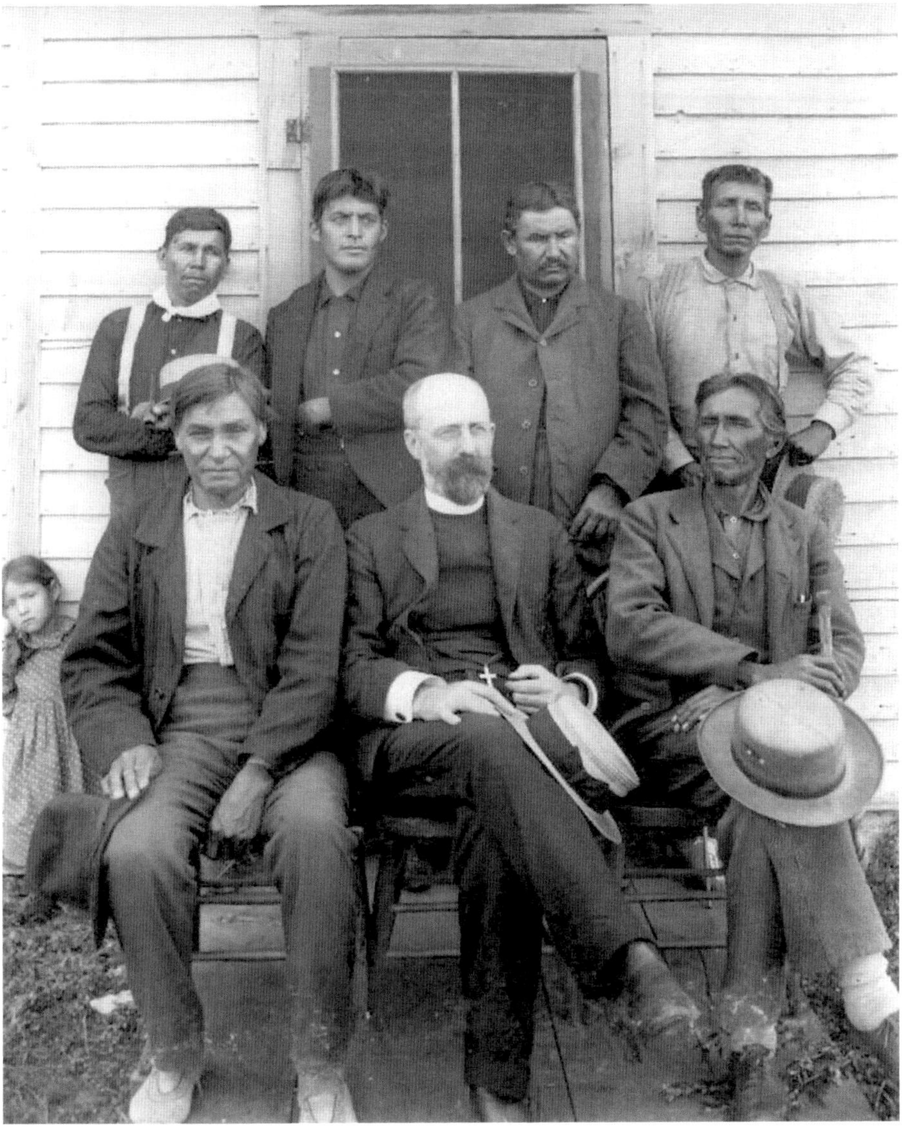

Dakota forced to wear European clothing sit with a man of God. *Courtesy of Gary Revier, Redwood Falls, Minnesota.*

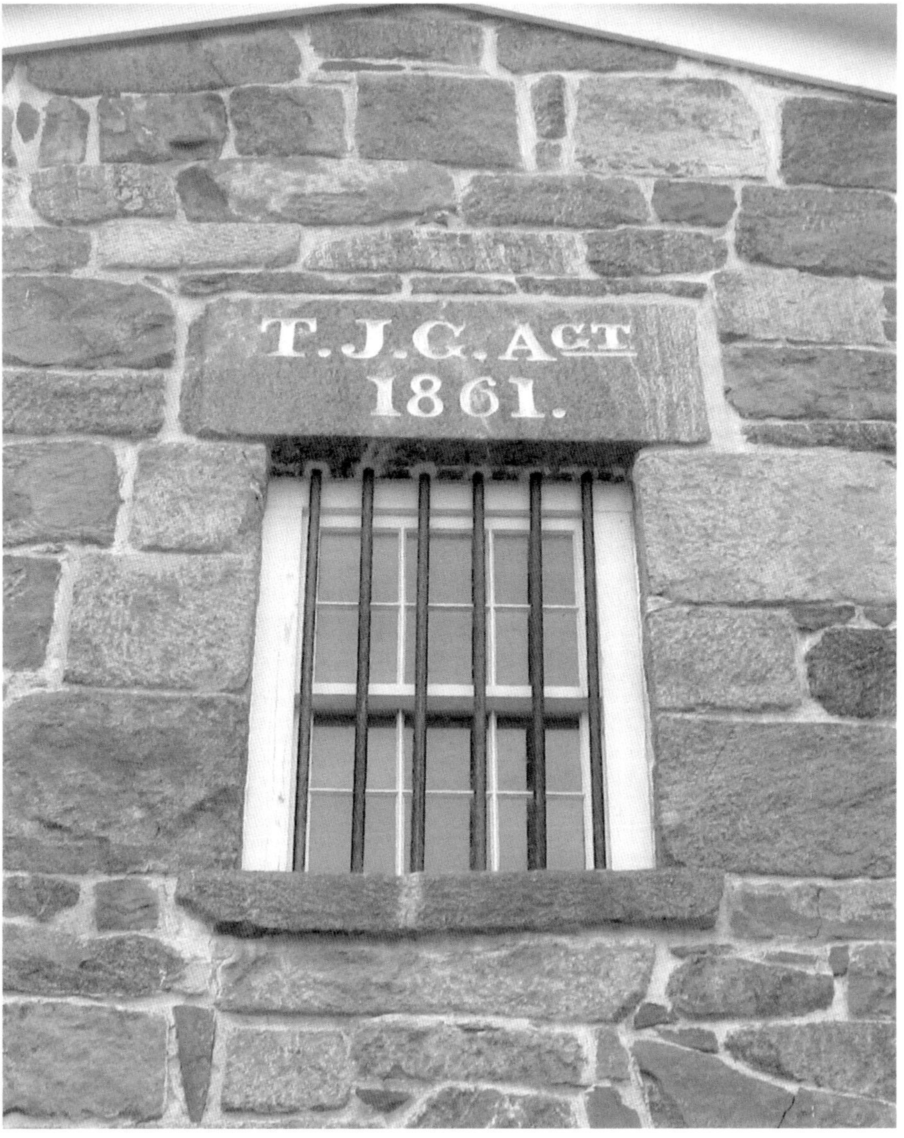

Stone bearing the initials of Thomas J. Galbraith, agent at the Lower Sioux Agency near Morton, Minnesota.

Putting the indigenous people's lives in danger from aggressive settlers helped force the eradication of the valley's native people and their culture. It was Ramsey's policies that freed up the fertile Minnesota River Valley for European pioneers to settle on.

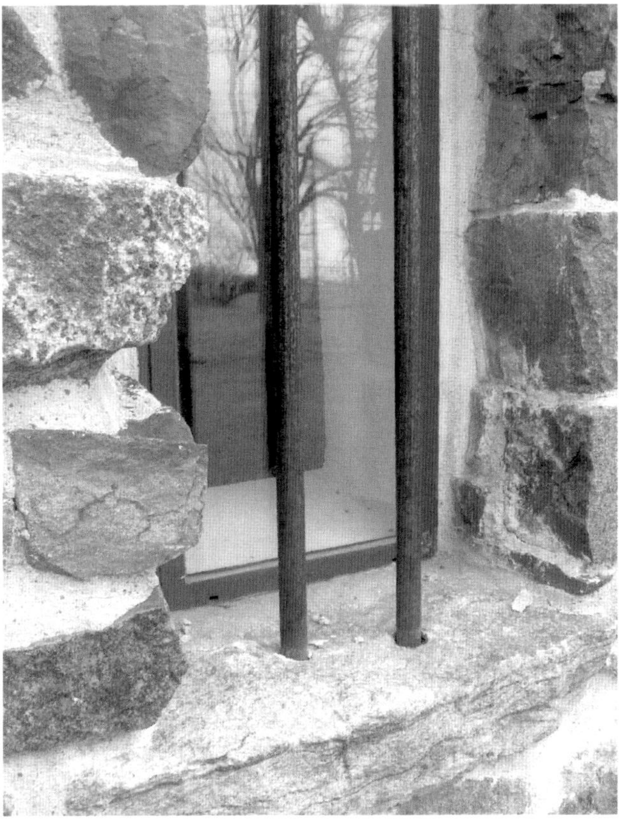

Barred window on the stone warehouse that held undistributed food intended for the starving Native Americans the summer of 1862.

Treaty of Old Crossing, 1863

After the U.S.-Dakota Conflict ended in 1863, the treaties that had been signed in 1851 were renegotiated by Ramsey. The Native American chiefs unwillingly ceded more land to the government. Ramsey made no provision for payment of debt that Indians were forced to owe to fur traders in the original treaties. But immediately after signing, natives were "pulled by the blankets" to sign a separate paper acknowledging such debts and authorizing payments from the annuities. Funds intended as payment to the surviving members of the tribes were thereby transferred from the Indians to the fur traders, who enjoyed a strong lobby in our state's government.

Ramsey bullied the tribes into signing the amended treaties with intimidation, bringing with him a cavalcade of 290 soldiers from Fort Snelling, hundreds of mules, horses and oxen and ninety vehicles and wagons. A Gatling gun was trained on the attending Native Americans, and Ramsey threatened temporary suspension of annuity payments.

Ramsey and his fellow negotiators fraudulently described the 1863 treaty as a request for the "right of passage" over tribal lands and succeeded in securing the property rights for the United States government.

Activists acting in the interest of the Native Americans objected to these amendments. The press attacked Ramsey for his role in treaty affairs, accusing him of fraud, but he was eventually found innocent.

Washington Social Life from 1863 to 1875

Ramsey resigned his governorship when he was elected as a Republican U.S. senator. He served in the Thirty-ninth through Forty-third Congresses. Later, under President Rutherford B. Hayes, Ramsey served as secretary of war from 1879 to 1881.

As a U.S. senator, Ramsey, his wife and their surviving daughter enjoyed Washington, D.C. social life. Personal papers preserved by the Minnesota Historical Society include descriptions of visits to wounded Civil War soldiers, dinners, receptions, trips and even the mention of Mrs. Ramsey attending the theatre with Mary Todd Lincoln in early 1865. The papers also detail an invitation from the secretary of war to Senator Ramsey inviting him to accompany Lincoln's funeral train to Springfield, Illinois, later that year.

Change of Heart or Irony?

Perhaps Ramsey had a change of heart in the years following his tenure as governor of Minnesota and started rethinking his position on minorities. Or perhaps he felt affection for African Americans because of the years when a beloved black woman served him and his family. Whatever the reason, Ramsey's later years seem to have been lived out by a kinder man.

On April 5, 1880, the only black cadet at West Point, Johnson C. Whittaker, was found in his room, immobilized from injuries suffered during an assault by fellow cadets. Ramsey brought the assault to the attention of President Hayes. An investigation concluded that West Point was a hotbed of snobbery and racism. Upon publication of these preliminary findings, there was a rush to reform the academy. But shortly before his graduation, Whittaker was dropped from the academy's roles for failing a final examination.

In the spring of 1880, Ramsey was invited to address the West Point graduating class. Ramsey shared the message that it is "ignoble to be governed by an imagined superiority and thrice ignoble to make active exhibition of so unworthy a sentiment by oppressing those we may deem beneath us. A true manhood dictates the extending of a helping hand."

In the end, Ramsey was applauded for his humanity in a letter from Martin I. Townsend, U.S. district attorney for the northern district of New York. The correspondence praises Ramsey for "saying kind words and doing kind deeds for the weak and friendless."

Ramsey passed away on April 22, 1903, and was buried in the Oakland Cemetery in St. Paul, Minnesota.

The Double Hanging of William Rose

Quite a few years ago, I worked for a business that required me to use a till. The only employees making change were my supervisor and me. During the course of our shift, a customer paid with a $100 bill. I don't recall which of us received that bill, but it was my supervisor who placed it under the tray in the drawer of the till. At the end of the day, when my supervisor was counting the cash in order to balance the books, he lifted the tray to retrieve the big bill and discovered that it was missing. He looked at me, and I looked at him.

Now, it had never occurred to me that my supervisor may have slipped the bill out of the till when I wasn't looking, but I could tell from the look on his face that he did not have the same faith in me. I was in a pickle. I couldn't imagine how I was going to prove that I hadn't taken that $100 bill. He looked in the till again and again, and finally the bill came unstuck from the bottom of the coin tray and he had it in his hand. I can still recall my sense of helplessness as I stood there silently accused.

I suppose my moment of panic is a poor comparison to that of William Rose, the only man to die for a crime in Redwood County. But I am certainly sympathetic because, you see, I don't believe Rose was guilty. I believe it was a case of mistaken identity, or a setup, in the murder of Moses Lufkin back on August 22, 1888.

I've read several accounts of the trial, and I cannot be convinced, beyond a reasonable doubt, that Rose murdered Lufkin. The story goes something like this: on the fateful night of the murder, Rose's neighbors, the Eli Slovers

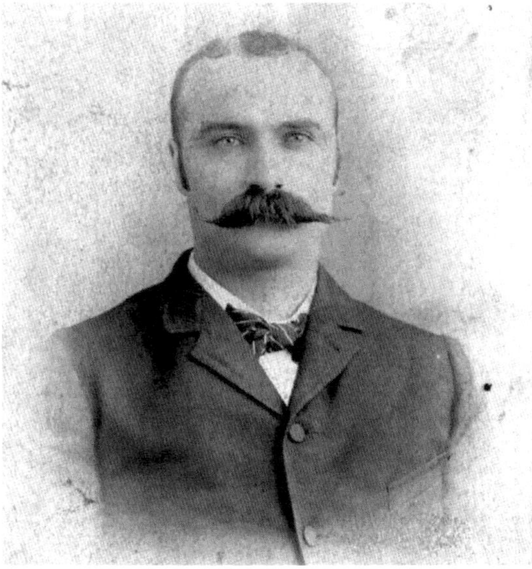

Portrait of William Rose, taken the day before his execution in 1891 in Redwood Falls, Minnesota.

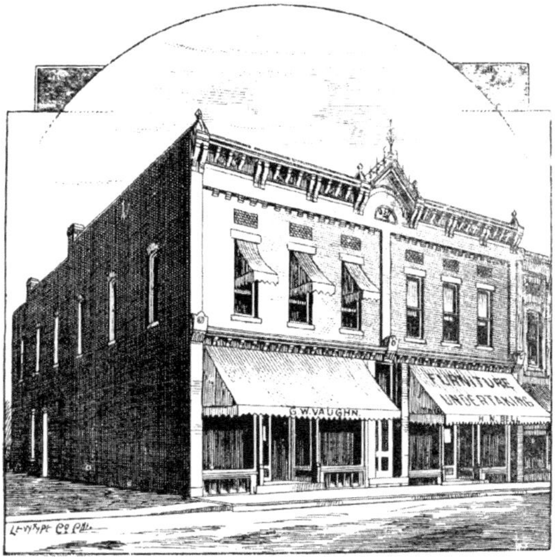

Bell's Undertaking, where William Rose selected his own casket in Redwood Falls. *Courtesy of Gary Revier, Redwood Falls, Minnesota.*

from Gales Township near Tracy, were visiting with Mrs. Slover's uncle, Moses Lufkin. Lufkin had recently sold his farm and was staying on as a guest with the family.

It was about a quarter past eight o'clock on a hot summer evening. In hopes of catching a cool breeze through the open living room window, the Slover children, Clara and Tennessee, joined their parents and Great-Uncle Moses for a visit.

Deader than Hay

The visit soon turned to chaos, however, when they were astonished by the blast of a gun. Lufkin slumped to the floor, where he is quoted as moaning, "Help. Come quick! I have been shot through the body, killed deader than hay."

Eli Slover later testified that he ran to the window, where he observed a bullet hole in the screen and someone, who may have been William Rose, running toward the grove. He said he thought it was Rose.

So what reason would Rose have to kill Lufkin? Well, it seems that Lufkin had brought a suit against the Rose family, accusing them of slander, and at the time of the murder, Lufkin was awaiting the results of that case. And then there was the matter of Rose's interest in the Slovers' twenty-year-old daughter, Grace, who for reasons unknown was sent to Chicago to live with an older married sister. Rose had been courting Grace, but the courtship had been broken off. If Rose had been jilted or prevented from seeing Grace, wouldn't he have shot Mr. and Mrs. Slover instead? Based upon Slover's testimony, a warrant was issued for Rose's arrest, and he was picked up and jailed.

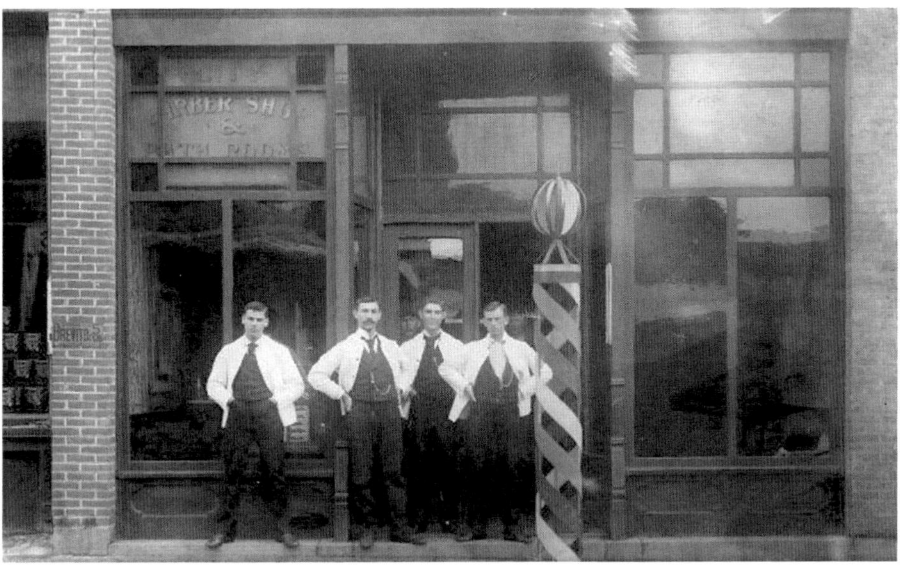

The barbershop where William Rose got his hair cut the day before his hanging. *Courtesy of Gary Revier, Redwood Falls, Minnesota.*

The case becomes even more questionable when testimony brings up an exchange between Slover and his daughter immediately after the gunfire. She warned her father not to go near the window, lest he be shot. "No," he told her, "they've shot their man." Did Slover hire someone to kill his wife's uncle? Why was he so sure he was safe?

Rose's defense team was made up of a prominent lawyer from St. Paul and F.S. Brown, an attorney from Tracy. Judging the case was B.F. Weber, who hailed from New Ulm along the Minnesota River to the east.

Evidence against Rose was highly problematic. For instance, two additional witnesses were only able to testify that they had seen a man with a build similar to Rose's riding a buckskin horse similar to Rose's. In addition, a compelling piece of evidence was a set of footprints left beneath the window from which the gun had been fired.

In an effort to defend himself, Rose added more fuel to the fire. He told the court he had ridden to his uncle's farm at the time of the shooting to deliver a box of bullets. The problem was that although his uncle corroborated the story, he denied having any idea why bullets were brought to him, or that he had requested them. Was Rose's uncle the murderer?

A bit of evidence brought up in Rose's favor was the defense that the hoof prints believed to have been left by the murderer's horse appeared unshod, and Rose's horse had shoes on its front hooves.

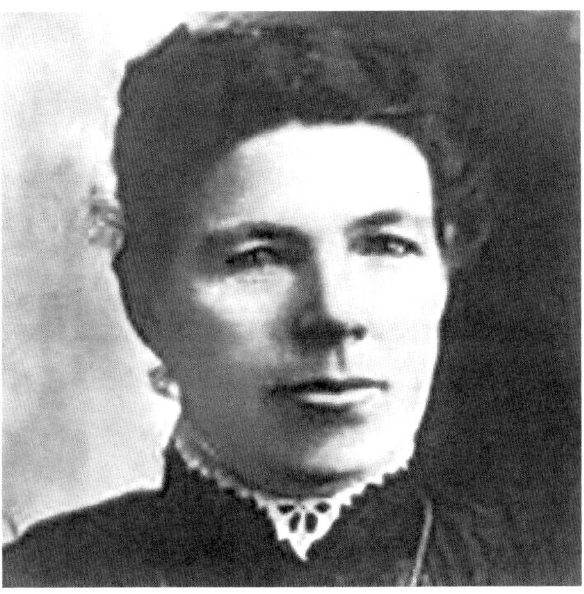

"Moustache Maude," sister of convicted murderer William Rose, who was re-hanged after the rope he was hanged from broke during his execution in 1891.

After two and a half days and three nights, the jury was unable to conclude without a reasonable doubt that Rose was guilty. As a result of their doubt, a new trial was set for May 9, 1889. The second trial met with similar results. The jury heard all of the evidence, but this time, the prosecutor was able to produce witnesses who swore Rose had threatened Lufkin's life. Still, Slover could not positively identify Rose as the shooter. The jury mulled over the new evidence from Thursday evening until the following Tuesday but remained split, and a third trial was scheduled for November 12, 1889.

It seems the only people available, or willing, to vouch for Rose were family members. And what a family!

Moustache Maude

William Rose had a number of siblings, but none was more colorful than his baby sister, Clara Belle, born in 1873. Clara Belle was a rambunctious child who was devoted to her father but often ran into disputes with her mother.

At the age of fifteen, while her parents were away, Clara Belle loaded a wagon with grain, hitched a team of horses to it, hauled her bounty to the local grain elevator and sold it, pocketing the money. She left the wagon and team at the livery stable and hitched a ride to the Twin Cities, over one hundred miles to the east.

Clara Belle moved in with her sister, Dora, who lived in Minneapolis, and spent the next six or seven years at several different jobs. She waited on tables and eventually trained as a seamstress for a tailor. After saving a substantial amount of money, Clara Belle traveled to South Dakota to work in her brother John's hotel. She waited tables but proved, at the age of twenty-three, to be an astute businesswoman with a gut sense for business. She saved enough money to establish a saloon in Winona, North Dakota, across the Missouri River from Fort Yates on the Standing Rock Reservation, where liquor was outlawed.

Though an attractive woman, Clara Belle developed a moustache, which she had removed at the barbershop and which earned her the nickname "Moustache Maude." Maude dressed in practical men's clothing, strapping a six-shooter to her leg to maintain peace in her saloon and brothel. She rolled her own cigarettes, smoking constantly. Maude provided a haven for fallen women, eventually becoming a midwife and claiming to have "smacked half of the bottoms in the county."

In the fall of 1897, while herding cattle near Mobridge in the Dakota Territory, a Texan named Arthur Pierce "Otto" Black headed into the wild little town of Winona for adventure. There he met and fell in love with twenty-four-year-old Moustache Maude, and the couple was married but later divorced.

Maude is believed to be the only woman in the country convicted of cattle rustling. She was brought to trial in 1924 in St. Theresa's Hall at Fort Yates, accused of butchering a cow and calf that wandered back to her ranch after she had sold them to an Indian. The sale made them government cows with an Indian number brand. Though convicted, she served no sentence for her crime.

Moustache Maude is now a revered part of Standing Rock history and was nominated for induction into the North Dakota Cowboy Hall of Fame.

Rose Meets "Spooky" Merriam

Working as a hunting guide and scout for his brother's business in Lake Kampeska, South Dakota, William Rose was hired by an ambitious St. Paul, Minnesota banker and avid sportsman, William Rush "Spooky" Merriam. Merriam later became a politician whose most memorable accomplishments included his ability to convince Congress to establish a permanent Census Bureau and adopt the Australian ballot, giving voters the opportunity to vote in relative privacy.

Merriam was also remembered as being good-natured and having an attractive personality. In spite of his delightful countenance, Rose and "Spooky" got into a passionate argument and duked it out, parting in anger. This was one bridge that Rose would regret burning.

Rose Goes on Trial for a Third Time

A man with the reputation for having been the greatest Minnesota criminal lawyer of the century was brought in from St. Paul to aid in the defense of Rose in his third, and final, trial. William W. Erwin, known for his expertise in homicide cases, studied the crime but later admitted that the Rose case stumped him. Slover eventually made a positive identification of Rose, and the jury agreed unanimously to a guilty verdict.

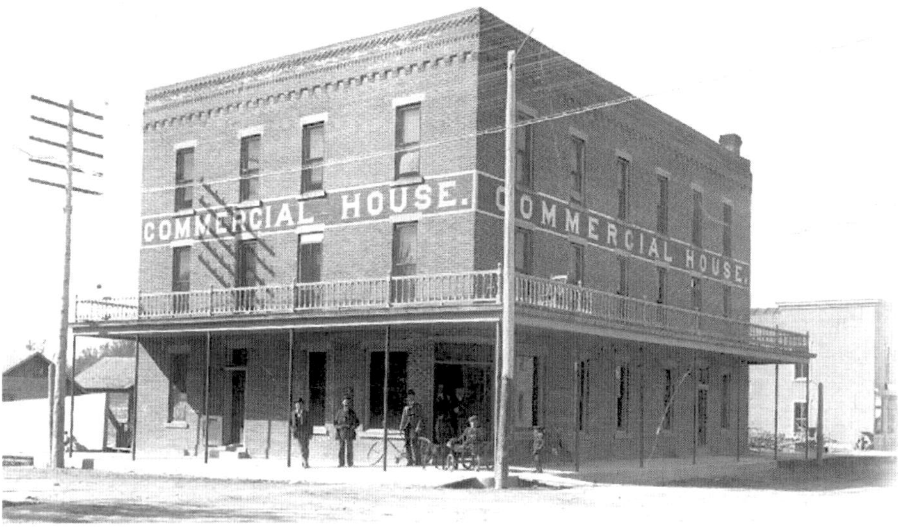

The Commercial House where William Rose ate his final meal. *Courtesy of Gary Revier, Redwood Falls, Minnesota.*

Judge Weber ordered Rose to be "hanged by the neck until dead," and the new governor of the state of Minnesota, a gentleman by the name of William Rush "Spooky" Merriam, was to set the date. An execution date of April 11, 1890, was set. In May of that year, Grace Lufkin took her own life by slashing her throat with a razor.

Rose maintained his innocence throughout the entire trial and during the time it took to appeal the decision with the Supreme Court. His appeal was denied, and Governor Merriam decided to wade through the trial evidence himself.

Merriam was also studying the details of a trial for another man, Clifton Holden, accused of murdering Frank Dodge near Redwood Falls. The Holden and Rose murder trials ran in parallel, and the accused were often handcuffed together and transported from jail to court together. Dodge was also found guilty of murder, but he had never gone toe to toe with the governor of Minnesota in a fight. As a result, Merriam commuted Holden's death sentence, but in regard to Rose, he said, "Let that @#%* hang!"

HANGED TWICE

Governor Merriam ordered Rose to be hanged on October 16, 1891. The day before he was to hang, he had his photograph taken at N.B. Anderson's studio in Redwood Falls. He asked that the photos be given to a number of individuals. One was a young woman he had met while housed in the New Ulm jail, "if she wished it." She became extremely distraught and verbal when she was denied a visit before Rose's execution. Another photo he wanted given to his parents, along with a letter maintaining his innocence.

The day of his hanging, Rose was awakened at 4:00 a.m. He cooperated with his jailers and, for his last meal, ordered oysters and eggs. A new law excluded all but official witnesses from observing an execution. However, a large crowd gathered near the enclosure securing the gallows in an alley northwest of the courthouse. Reporters from the Twin Cities were on hand to record the event.

Rose told his executioners to "watch Slover" during the hanging. He then proceeded up the steps of the gallows and directed the sheriff to "do his duty" while the sheriff placed the rope around his neck. What happened

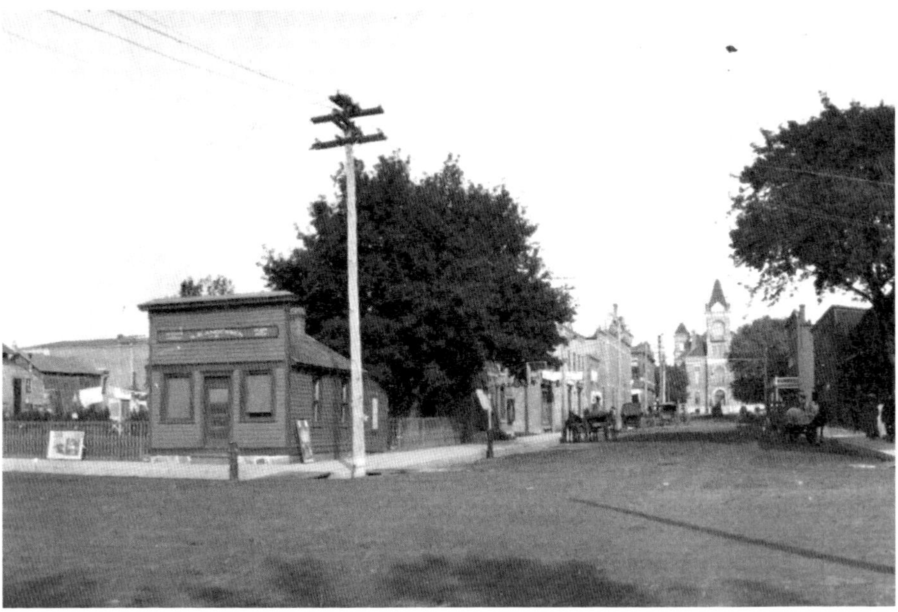

The Anderson Studio where William Rose had his last picture taken. *Courtesy of Gary Revier, Redwood Falls, Minnesota.*

next is cruel and unusual. When the trapdoor dropped and Rose was jerked by the rope, it suddenly snapped, and Rose fell to the ground, unconscious. He was hauled back up the steps, over the sheriff's shoulder, and hanged by a second rope, taking his sweet time to die.

A Twin Cities newspaper reported the hanging as "more of a hog-killing than a judicial execution." And the local newspaper declared, "Heaven forbid that Redwood County have another murder or execution soon." Rose's body was taken back to his hometown of Tracy for burial. As far as "watching Slover" goes, Rose's words have left a veneer of doubt on the whole affair. Guilty, or not guilty?

C.O. Gilfillan

A Rich Man with a Big Heart

Summertime was a different experience for small-town kids than it was for us out on the farm. For one thing, I complained, town kids didn't have to get up at the crack of dawn to work in the fields or milk cows. I envied my schoolmates in tiny nearby Wabasso, riding past them in an old green station wagon crammed with my family and groceries, my cheek resting against the car window.

In the yard of the little brick library, donated by a gentleman named C.O. Gilfillan, kids waited in their swimsuits, with towels draped over their arms, for the school bus that would drive them to swimming lessons in a clear, chlorine-scented pool one town away.

My siblings and I grumbled under the blazing summer sun, walking through miles and miles of soybean fields, pulling spiky thistle and getting our fingers glued together with sticky, white milkweed goo. My old dad said he could hear us arguing all the way up at the farm site. But the truth is, we didn't work half as hard as some of our neighbors.

I was lucky to have grown up near Daub's Lake, a modest body of water surrounded by trees and cattails. At the end of the day, when our work was done, my siblings and I hiked a quarter mile or so to a spot we called "the swimming area." Someone had generously dumped a load of pea rock and sand in a clearing for a bit of beach and built an outhouse in the trees. Stones, probably collected from our fields, ringed a cold fire pit waiting for the next marshmallow roast.

On our hikes back and forth to the lake, we'd entertain ourselves by trying to catch dust devils spinning across the field like little tornadoes, jumping through their dusty funnels, an especially dirty business if we were still damp from our swim.

Remembering those long, hot summers gives me a special appreciation for the stories of kindness toward the women and children of Paxton Township attributed to C.O. Gilfillan. His vast, red-roofed estate near the community of Morgan lay just outside the Minnesota River Valley. Books are filled with stories of great men and their fortunes, among which Gilfillan would be counted. But in my opinion, the true test of greatness is the willingness to share the spoils of fortune.

C.O. GILFILLAN

Charles Oswin Gilfillan was the son of Charles Duncan Gilfillan, the main person credited with bringing clean water to the city of St. Paul, Minnesota,

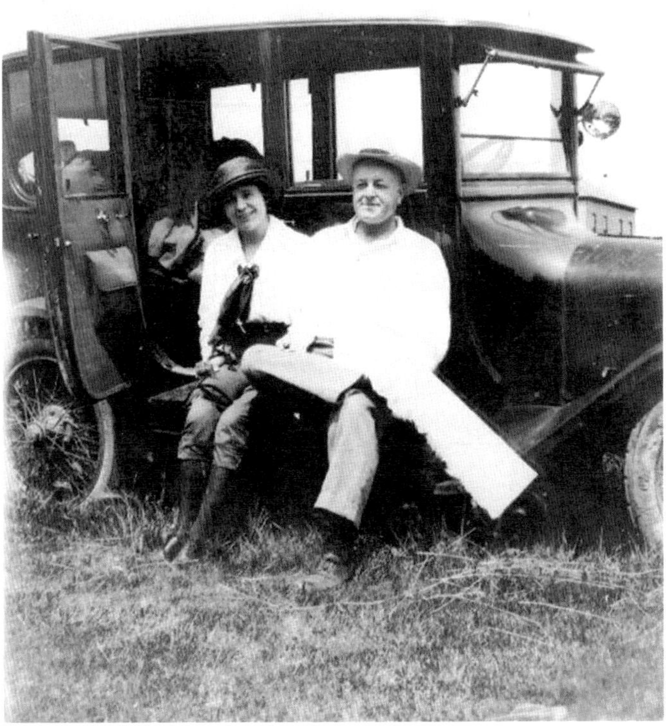

C.O. and Anne Gilfillan in the early 1900s. *Courtesy of Gary Revier, Redwood Falls, Minnesota.*

in 1870. Charles D. was a lawyer, politician, entrepreneur and historian. He was a friend and contemporary of the famous James J. Hill.

The senior Gilfillan was very interested in the events of the U.S.-Dakota Conflict of 1862 and, in 1894, became chairman of a committee appointed by the state legislature to erect a monument marking the Battle of Birch Coulee. On February 2, 1895, he helped organize and became president of the Minnesota Valley Historical Society, whose main mission was to identify and erect markers at the most significant battle sites. Charles D. invested thousands of his own dollars to complete the mission. Though the prose and names etched into the markers tend to neglect the names and suffering of the indigenous people, they nevertheless remain as a reminder and point of discussion for visitors and historians.

But here's the Gilfillan story I find most intriguing. During the Great Depression, in the summer of 1933, C.O. Gilfillan invited thirty-eight teenaged boys from Paxton Township to enjoy a four-day vacation at Green Lake near Spicer, Minnesota. The boys went on vacation, eight at a time, and were supervised by one of Gilfillan's assistants. Lucky boys! The following year, the moms and daughters had a chance to see what a vacation was like, all at Gilfillan's expense.

In 1937, Gilfillan, edging toward his sixty-fifth birthday, created the Charles D. Gilfillan Paxton Memorial Fund in honor of his father. The fund

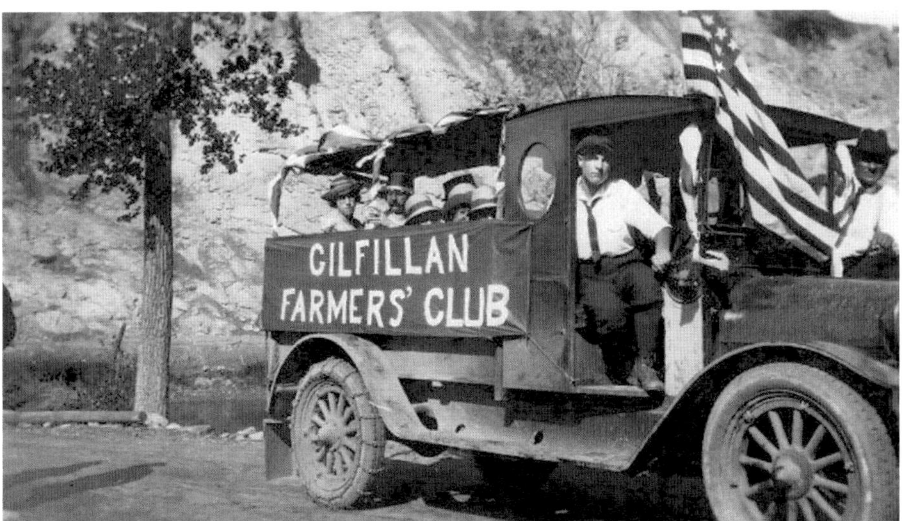

An outing hosted by C.O. and Anne Gilfillan in the early 1900s. *Courtesy of Gary Revier, Redwood Falls, Minnesota.*

was to be managed by a board of five members, including his wife, Anna. The mission of the fund was to plan anything that made the lives of their Paxton Township neighbors more pleasant. In addition, money was used to buy uniforms for the local kitten ball team; host speakers, entertainers and outings; and give the women and children of Paxton Township respite from the summer heat with trips to the lake.

The first Paxton Township event hosted by the fund was a gala at the armory in neighboring Redwood Falls. The board hired a personality from the Twin Cities to emcee. Families were treated to music by an eight-piece orchestra and entertainment by acrobats, singers, dancers, a magician and others. In the evening the adults attended a dance and played cards. There is little doubt that this extravaganza, attended by more than four hundred people, would have been the highlight of the winter in snowy Minnesota farm country.

The foundation board continued planning and hosting events for years. Oh, to be a member of Paxton Township and the recipient of the goodwill extended to ordinary citizens by a man who saw joy in sharing his good fortune with others.

Farming Innovations

C.D. Gilfillan purchased his land in the 1880s after disposing of his Ramsey County property. This was a decade after Redwood County was devastated by the grasshopper infestation recorded in Laura Ingalls Wilder's book *On the Banks of Plum Creek*. Ingalls lived, at the time, near Walnut Grove in the southern end of the county.

The three-hundred-pound senior Gilfillan was interested in the innovation of new farming techniques, proving top-quality beef could be raised as far north as Minnesota. That idea had been previously laughed at by men in the Chicago stockyards and appreciated by local farmers who preferred cattle to a rich man's pasture full of fancy horses.

Gilfillan tackled the weedy pastures without a plow, sowing seed on top of native prairie grass and giving his livestock waves of grass to wade in for fattening. He fed his livestock corn in the winter, and his cattle became well known for their quality.

The senior Gilfillan also planted thousands of trees for beautification and windbreaks. He made sure that his fields were well fertilized with manure and his crops were rotated to keep the land from wearing out. He used the latest machinery, always ready for the next innovation.

C.O. Gilfillan

The younger Gilfillan, C.O., was interested in becoming a doctor but, at his father's urging, attended the University Farm School in St. Paul in preparation for the next generation of farming. Rather than running the acreage as one huge stock farm, like his father, C.O. partitioned the land off into smaller parcels with well-maintained, red-roofed houses and outbuildings. Settlers were encouraged to move onto the land, and a farming community was begun.

Years later, during the Depression of the 1930s, when corn prices fell to eight cents a bushel and over 125 farms in Redwood County were foreclosed on, C.O.'s farmers fared better than most. Gilfillan purchased their crops for twice the market rate, storing the grain for sale at a later date, when prices increased. C.O.'s efforts to help his farmers succeed endeared him to renters on Gilfillan land. The family was interested in developing a healthy farming community.

A story in the book *Like Father, Like Son—The Gilfillan Story*, by Merrill E. Jarrow, tells of Anna and C.O.'s return from their Chicago honeymoon in the fall of 1920. The couple was surprised to find four hundred members of the Redwood Falls and Morgan communities, complete with community band, greeting them at their estate. It was a testament to the generosity and goodwill sown by two generations of Gilfillans.

Many of the attendees were residents of Gilfillan farms. The reception influenced the partygoers, who soon coordinated the Gilfillan Farmer's Club. The group met for the first time on March 22, 1921, with social and financial objectives. Gilfillan offered cash prizes to encourage excellence in farming and to give families an opportunity to hear music and lectures and enjoy the society of one another.

The Gilfillan Estate became a gathering place.

Farmfest

Flash forward to the first Farmfest, held in 1972. The event was hatched on the Burt Hanson farm in southeastern Minnesota, when the World Ploughing Contest was held in the United States for the first time in the event's history. Representatives from twenty-nine countries, including farmers near Vernon Center, participated. The Hanson farm hosted the exhibition.

Several years later, Farmfest was held on the Les Lloyd farm near Lake Crystal, Minnesota, celebrating the Bicentennial Salute to Agriculture in the United States. The event also noted the arrival of the twenty-six-car Bicentennial Freedom Train on its trip across the forty-eight contiguous states. Farmfest lasted a week and included performances by some of the biggest names in entertainment.

The event was plagued by bad weather and a host of other difficulties, bringing the festival to bankruptcy. In 1977, entrepreneur Marlyn Buss purchased the Farmfest name from the bankruptcy court and brought the event to his father's farm east of Lake Crystal, Minnesota. Buss scaled the event back to three days and emphasized agriculture over entertainment. Farmfest grew steadily and was soon too large for his father's farm, prompting a move to Austin, Minnesota, where it was hosted for another four years.

In 1994, Farmfest was moved to the historic Gilfillan farm. There, the ghosts of celebrations past can once again enjoy the society of farmers and innovation during three days of festivities and food for the entire family.

The Gilfillan Estate is now lovingly managed by the Redwood County Historical Society.

WABASSO LIBRARY

I have to confess an uncomfortable memory of the white-columned, classic brick- and slate-roofed library built by C.O. Gilfillan in Wabasso, in the heart of Redwood County. Back when I was young, Wabasso had a tradition of keeping its stores open until 9:00 p.m. on Fridays. I recall enchanting summer evenings in town. Looking back, I realize I was experiencing the epitome of small-town charm.

The community band performed in good weather, seated on a raised wooden platform supported by barrels. The band played John Philip Sousa selections and other rousing music. My older brother, Steve, and a couple of cousins, Mike and Mark (whom my twin brother Jeff and I pronounced "Mike" and "Mowk" until we perfected our *R*s), played in the brass section. Afterward, they each received a ticket for a free bottle of pop.

The town was packed with farmers and townspeople on Friday evenings, some sitting in their cars listening to the band, honking their horns in appreciation after each song. We'd often run into town kids we knew from school. I was grateful to be off the farm and in civilization.

One of those Fridays when I was in grade school, I checked the book *Charlotte's Web* out of the library. I printed my name neatly on the card and tucked the book under my arm. When I got home, I read it over and over again. And then one day, to my horror, I realized I had forgotten to return it by the due date stamped in the back of the book. I panicked.

I had committed a crime, and I was afraid to tell anyone. I didn't have any money of my own to pay a fine, and I was pretty sure I would be scolded for being irresponsible, so I tried to destroy the evidence, hoping no one would notice. My plan lacked a certain amount of foresight and common sense.

My first attempt at hiding the book was an act of genius. My dad was remodeling our dark, narrow stairway leading to the second floor by taking out the top part of the wall. As a result, I was able to simply drop the book down between the two-by-fours. I assumed dad would finish the rough edges of the wall with a nice piece of lumber, and no one would be the wiser.

That wasn't, of course, what happened. I heard him laugh his loud laugh and hold the book over his head saying, "How did this get down there?" Drat. I took the book from him and hauled it back up to my room. I lost sleep planning my next attempt to cover up my heinous crime.

I was getting desperate. This time, I waited until I was sure no other kids were around, and I took the book out to the pit where we burned our garbage. I thought I had concealed it fairly well and that it would be consumed by flames the next time Dad burned the garbage. But all of a sudden, here came my dad walking up to the house, shaking his head, wondering how the same book he had pulled out of the wall ended up in the garbage.

I guess he must have returned the book to the library for me, and thank goodness he did, for I had my eye on a copy of *Snip, Snap & Snur*. No one ever mentioned it again.

Gilwood Haven

There is a story about C.O. Gilfillan that has endeared him to me and to the mothers of two previous generations. The setting of the tale is a cold and windy Saturday night in the winter of 1937 when C.O. was conducting business in Redwood Falls. The temperature was below zero, and in the streets he observed mothers with their small children having nowhere to go for comfort while their husbands completed their business.

He observed the children, lips blue with cold, hanging on their mothers' skirts, and saw young women slipping into cold automobiles to feed their babies. C.O. shared his observations with his wife, and they agreed that the city needed a women's lounge where mothers and children would be safe and warm while their husbands shopped and took care of business. The building would also include city offices and a public bathroom on the lower level.

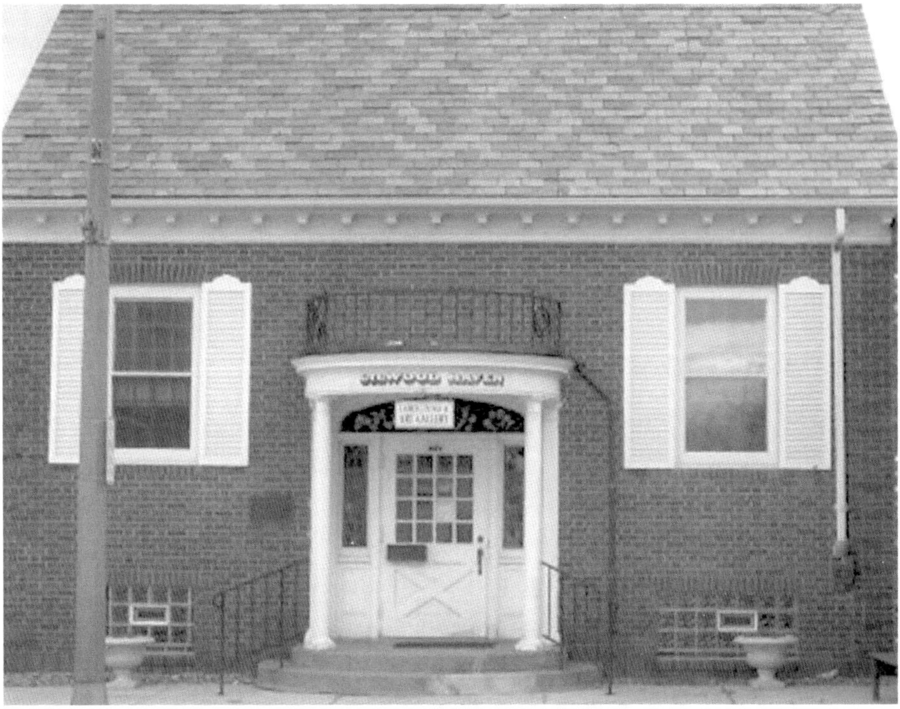

Gilwood Haven, built by C.O. Gilfillan for women to care for their children in comfort while their husbands took care of business in downtown Redwood Falls in the early 1900s.

Three years later, on February 9, 1940, in front of a large crowd of appreciative community members, with the high school band playing, the city council accepted Gilwood Haven and eighty acres of land, from which the rent collected would be used to maintain the building and employ a matron to oversee its use. In less than two years, Gilwood Haven's guestbook recorded over eighty thousand guests from 371 communities, thirty-one states and three countries.

Historic Gilwood Haven remains open at 219 South Mill Street, available during daytime visits to Redwood Falls. It can be recognized by the Gilfillan signature white-columned, brick- and slate-roofed architecture.

Gilfillan Collection at the Morgan Library

Anna and C.O. Gilfillan continued to improve life in Redwood County with gifts of additional buildings. Upkeep was provided with acreage to be rented out for maintenance costs.

In 1938, nearby Morgan benefited extensively from the gift of a handsome brick building complete with a library, women's community space and museum. It was built with funds from the Public Works Administration and a grant from the Gilfillans. The museum on the lower level now holds Gilfillan memorabilia.

In addition, a generous donation by the Gilfillans made possible the construction of Gil-Mor Manor, a nursing home opened in 1961. The name of this distinctive building was selected through a contest hosted by the community.

Nearby Mountain Lake was also blessed with good fortune when the Gilfillans donated a significant amount of money toward the building of a hospital wing. And the city of Clements was also gifted with a smart brick municipal building.

C.O. Gilfillan passed away in his home on December 22, 1962, at the age of ninety while Ann was serving him breakfast. Ann followed later on July 7, 1990.

The Gilfillan Foundations continue to provide support to local residents finding it difficult to pay their medical bills in Paxton Township and throughout Minnesota, ensuring the legacy of the Gilfillans' generosity lives on.

Sears, Roebuck and Company's Serendipitous Start

When I was a little girl growing up on the southern Minnesota prairie, my siblings and I knew Christmas wasn't too far off when the J.C. Penney and Sears Roebuck holiday catalogues arrived in the mail. We'd scrabble to look at them, with the big kids generally having first dibs and us younger ones waiting until the excitement wore off to get our chance at them.

Bright, shiny objects, just waiting to find their way under our Christmas tree, filled the catalogue pages. I had my eye on an aqua-colored Easy Bake Oven that came with little packets of ingredients to whip up a batch of tiny cookies baked under the heat of a light bulb. The irony of my desire won't be lost on my family, who knows full well that my oven, today, stays perfectly clean due to lack of use. But I was little. I didn't know any better.

We weren't a wealthy family. We were accustomed to receiving hand-me-downs from cousins. The exception was Easter, when we'd make the fifteen-mile trip to Redwood Falls to purchase store-bought dresses and Easter bonnets for me and my little sister, Annie, and new dress shirts for the boys.

Had we driven through town to the eastern end of Redwood Falls and taken a left at Redwood County Highway 101, we would have found ourselves curving into the Minnesota River Valley, across railroad tracks and into tiny North Redwood.

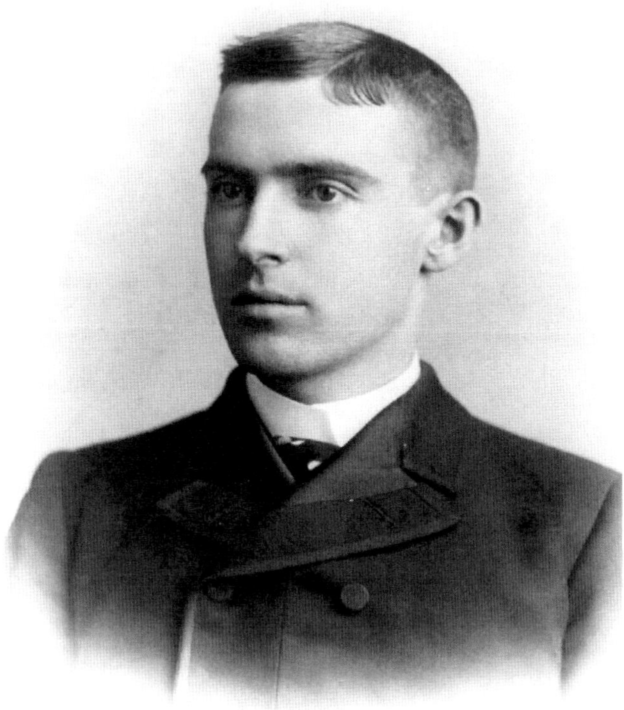

Richard Sears, founder of Sears and Roebuck, North Redwood, Minnesota. *Courtesy of Gary Revier, Redwood Falls, Minnesota.*

Richard Sears

In the late 1880s, twenty years after the native population lost the majority of their homelands in the heart-wrenching 1862 Dakota Conflict and pioneers were settling the prairie, Cadastral surveys were employed to divide the remaining public domain. Some of that land went to the railroads, which were making efficient movement of people and goods possible.

At the age of seventeen, an enterprising young man, Richard Sears, who was born in Stewartville, Minnesota, and who had learned telegraphy, became an agent for the Minneapolis and Saint Louis Railway station.

It's funny how life works. If not for local retailer Edward Stegerson refusing a shipment of watches from Chicago, Sears, Roebuck and Company might never have been founded.

In 1886, Stegerson was the victim of a then-common scam. A wholesaler would ship unrequested merchandise to a retailer at a premium price and then negotiate a discount, appearing to offset the cost of shipping. The

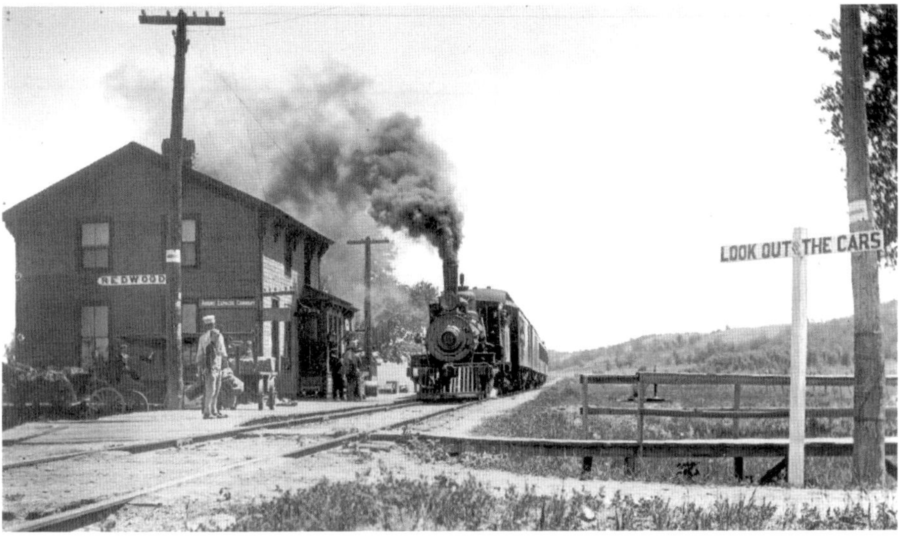

Depot in North Redwood where Richard Sears received the shipment of watches that started the Sears and Roebuck mail-order company in 1886. *Courtesy of Gary Revier, Redwood Falls, Minnesota.*

retailer would then re-price the products and sell them on commission, making a small profit.

Spotting an opportunity, Richard Sears contacted the wholesaler and got permission to sell the watches himself. Sears had a knack for knowing what type of products would sell as well as a gift for marketing and writing advertising copy that would appeal to the rural population. About the same time the watches arrived at the railway station in North Redwood, time zones, originally introduced by British railway companies in 1847, were being applied across the United States.

Within six months, Sears had made over $5,000 selling watches to other agents and passersby and decided to move to Minneapolis, Minnesota. There he began the R.W. Sears Watch Company.

Sears and Roebuck

In 1887, Sears moved his company to Chicago and hired a watch repairman, Curtis Roebuck, to attend to returned watches in need of repair. Six years into their relationship, the two men became partners and changed the name of the company to Sears, Roebuck and Company. Although the original

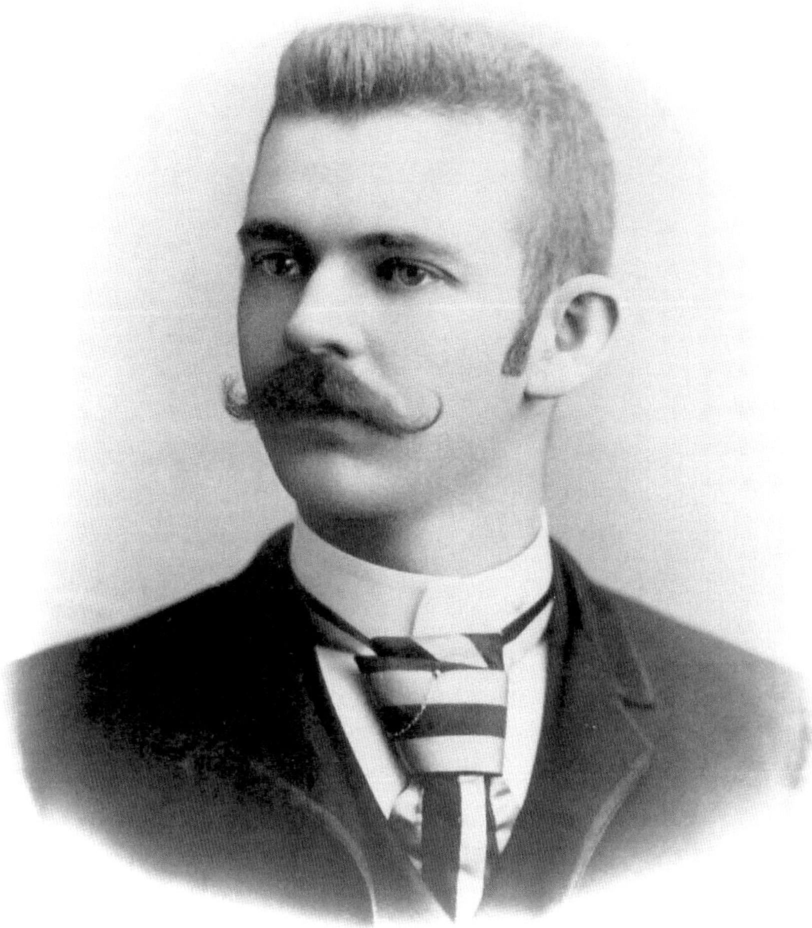

Alva Roebuck, Sears's business partner. *Courtesy of Gary Revier, Redwood Falls, Minnesota.*

catalogues featured only watches, Sears recognized the need to offer rural customers a variety of products. He began adding more catalogue items, including the ultimate purchase: a house.

Between 1908 and 1940, Sears offered almost 450 different housing styles and in a variety of price ranges. Once ordered, the lumber was cut and delivered for building. Sears houses continue to dot the countryside and provide sturdy homes for families in communities across Minnesota.

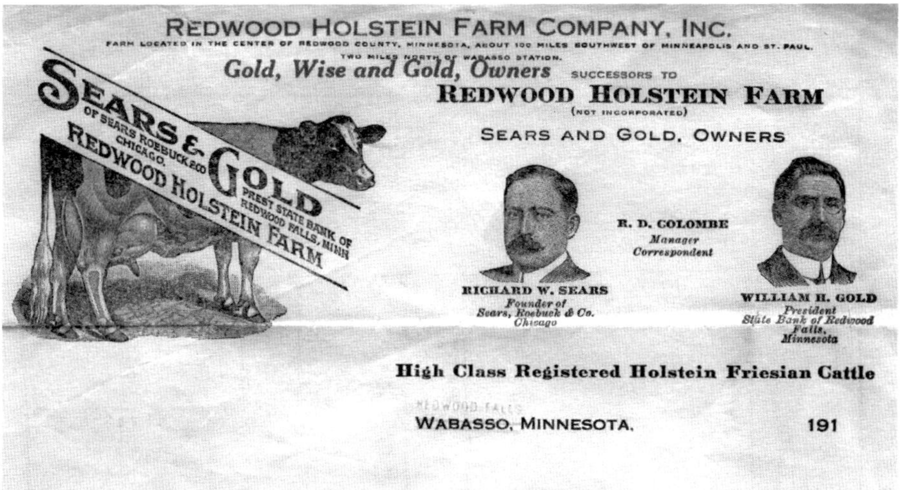

Stationery from Redwood Holstein Farm Company, Richard Sears's partnership with William Gold, Wabasso, Minnesota. *Courtesy of Gary Revier, Redwood Falls, Minnesota.*

Continued Involvement in Redwood County

Richard Sears maintained his interest in the Redwood area right up until his death in 1914. He financed Redwood Falls businesses by rebuilding part of the downtown after the big 1904 fire that destroyed the north side of Second Street. He also owned many farms in the area and maintained his local friendships. He was a well-known person on the streets and roads of Redwood Falls and the county.

His love of farming came from his father, who was a blacksmith with a dream of raising championship cattle. He lost his herd through disease, which broke his spirit and caused his premature death. Richard fulfilled his father's dream by raising cattle in Redwood County even after he had made his fortune in the retail business. Richard was in Redwood Falls the week before his death. His sisters stayed in the community for many years, one of them teaching in area schools. (It turns out that Sears's sisters were not the only teachers related to famous people who plied their professions in Redwood Falls. Two such similar people were Sinclair Lewis's mom and dad. His dad was principal and his mother a teacher.)

As for outdated Sears and Roebuck catalogues, many became outhouse staples after providing hours of entertainment and fodder for dreams.

The Myth about Scalping

Lunch with the Wabashas

Dear Diary,

Melanie and I traveled to southwestern Minnesota to visit with her good friends, Chief Ernest Wabasha and his beautiful wife, Vernell, at the Dacotah Ridge golf course, which, I was advised, is one of the finest courses in the state. It is surrounded by primitive river valley landscapes. We were also joined by a couple of engaging young women, Teri and Marisa, from the tribe's clinic, where Melanie worked years ago.

Melanie arranged the visit at my request, to help me get a sense of the Native American perspective of history in the Minnesota River Valley.

I felt a little bit like a groupie allowed backstage. Chief Wabasha looked stern and dignified, though when he spoke, he turned out to be a bit of a joker. You can see the kindness written all over his wife's face, and I wondered how they could approach life with such joy after hearing about the hurdles their nation has had to overcome to become the leaders they are today.

As for me, I felt very humbled and guilty by association with the white man. The truth of the Native American story is a hard one to listen to, and I don't believe we white kids have been given the stories straight. How did this group of people, terrorized by intruders and attempting to save their families and land, become known as savages? I'm just asking. But it seems like the lie we hear first is the story we remember, and it is a trick still being used today. Lie first, retract later. The damage is done.

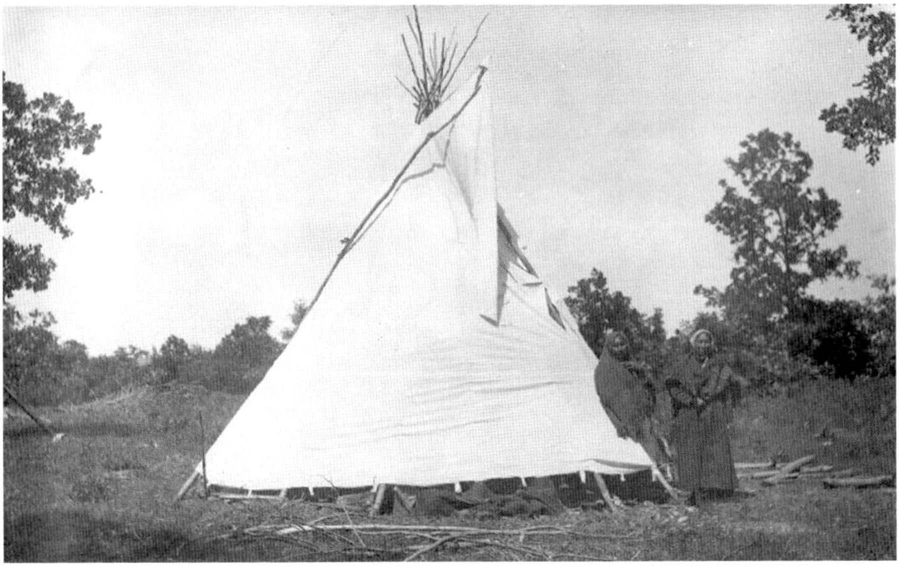

Vintage photograph of two Dakota women outside a tipi on the Lower Sioux Reservation. *Courtesy of Gary Revier, Redwood Falls, Minnesota.*

> *It's been years since the holocaust in the Minnesota River Valley that reduced the Native American population by roughly 95 percent, and it is clear many scars still remain. How could they not? But it seems that, even though we could expect to be viewed as a perpetual enemy of the tribes, they have wisely chosen, instead, to practice the art of forgiveness—which isn't the same as forgetting.*
>
> *Melanie asked what has changed the most in the Minnesota River Valley since white people have become stewards of the land, and Vernell stated it was the river itself. What once flowed clear and deep in a beautiful valley is now shallow and tired. Ever the optimist, I believe the pendulum will be swinging back. Bit by bit.*
>
> *I left our lunch saddened and enlightened, and thrilled to have just spent a couple of hours with the Wabashas. Darn. I should have asked for an autograph.*
>
> *—Minnesota Country Mouse*

When I was a farm girl, it was common practice to trap nuisance pocket gophers. The local township offered a twenty-five-cent-per-gopher bounty, awarded upon presenting a set of back gopher feet to the proper authorities. We often had jars of gopher feet accumulating in our freezer to be redeemed eventually for cash.

In my case, the payoff sum was typically mere coins because I wasn't very good at catching pocket gophers and kept my traps pretty close to home. My brothers, however, made a little money at it. The thought of setting a trap and cutting off gopher feet now leaves me feeling queasy, but at the time it didn't bother me at all.

This anecdote suggests two ideas. The first is that bounties are a part of American life. The second is that customs we once found tolerable we may now find abhorrent.

My whole life I have misunderstood the history and practice of scalping, until I met with Hereditary Chief Ernest Wabasha and his wife, Vernell. They are from the Mdewakanton Tribe at the Lower Sioux Reservation near Morton in southwestern Minnesota. In the course of the conversation, they advised me that scalping was not one of their customs.

"It wasn't?" I asked.

"No. It was introduced by the Europeans. We only did it in retribution for a death. And not only that, the United States government paid money for the scalp of an Indian," Chief Wabasha said.

This was news to me. So I headed home, started researching and, wouldn't you know it? They were right.

I had no idea that our government paid bounties for the scalps of human beings. This is the sad reality of life in the Minnesota River Valley in the 1860s. This abominable practice rolled across the country from the East Coast.

Scalping Encouraged by Europeans

European royalty introduced bounties, paying for the heads of their enemies, centuries before the practice migrated to the United States with the colonists. As far back as the eleventh century, the Earl of Wessex awarded bounties for the delivery of his enemies' severed heads. Remember the cry, "Off with their heads"?

Bounty hunting made for a profitable business with financial reward that few other occupations could offer. Just haul in your latest harvest of human heads to the government, have them tallied and leave with your pockets weighted heavy in gold. Thus the term "head count" came to be.

Beheading followed the Europeans into North America after Christopher Columbus arrived, and in an effort to clear the New World of indigenous people, it was eventually written into law. The colonists complained that heads were too cumbersome and smelly to store and haul to the authorities for payment. Eventually, they were allowed to redeem the scalp alone for reimbursement.

So whose scalps were these colonists gathering? In 1703, as the American colonies were being established, European authorities established the practice of collecting human heads. The law was first enacted in Massachusetts, offering sixty dollars for a male Native American scalp from an individual over the age of twelve.

The practice became popular and continued across the country to other colonies, and eventually the "powers that be" started paying for the scalps of indigenous women and children as well. The bloody scalps of the Native Americans led to the term "redskins."

Governor Ramsey Sanctions Murder

Research shows that ancient Native Americans practiced scalping to a small degree, typically in retribution for a murder. But it was the colonists who encouraged scalping and made it profitable.

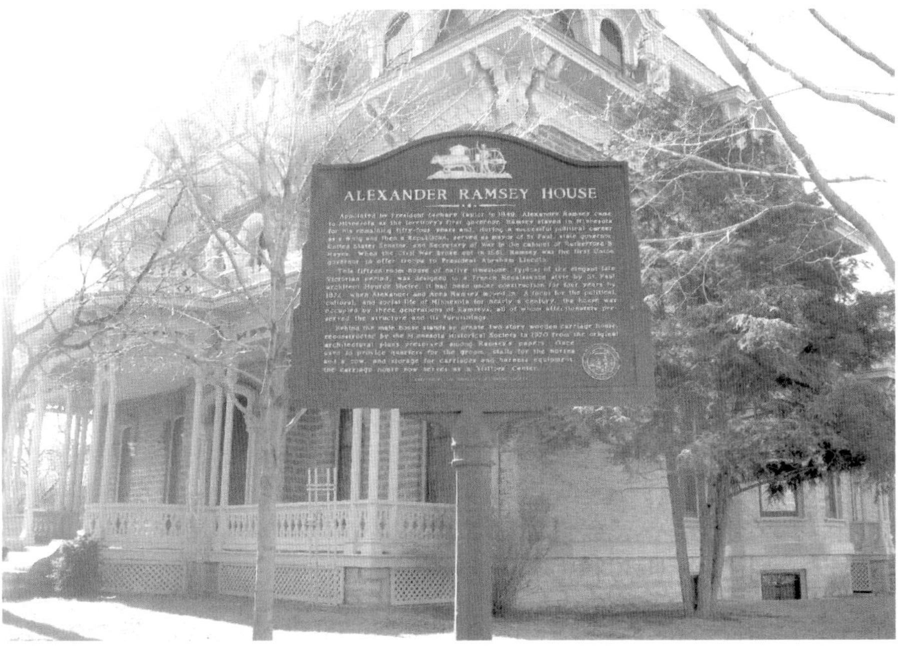

The Alexander Ramsey House in St. Paul, Minnesota.

If any doubt about the payment of bounties for the scalps of Native Americans remained, they were soon dispelled after reading the following article from the August 18, 1863 edition of the *New York Times*:

> *Waste of Warriors in the West*
> *The State of Minnesota, feeling aggrieved by the government's slow and humanitarian mode of conducting war against the hostile Indians within her borders, has lately adopted some very decisive but questionable measures of her own for getting rid of the "red devils."*
>
> *A proclamation appeared offering a State bounty for every "scalp" of a Sioux that should be brought in by volunteer and amateur hunters. The document rested upon the official authority of Gov. (now United States Senator) RAMSEY, and greatly shocked some of that gentleman's Eastern friends, who made haste (too much haste it seems) to repudiate the proclamation as a forgery and a slander.*
>
> *But later accounts confirm the authenticity of the original document, which, however, has since undergone some modification. The hunters of red-skins are no longer required to produce the scalps torn from the heads of slain victims, but must furnish "satisfactory affidavits" of their exploits in bringing down their human (or inhuman) game. A St. Paul correspondent of a contemporary gives the Minnesota view of the subject as follows:*
>
> *"Whatever exceptions humanitarians might take to the scalps bounty, they would soon be convinced of the wisdom and necessity of the present order if they would come among us, and expose their own scalps, instead of keeping at a safe distance, and prating about humanity. A 'Moral Minnesotian' is informed that he doesn't need to defend Senator RAMSEY from the imputations of issuing the order, as it is an act he is free to acknowledge, and ready to sustain."*
>
> *It is undoubtedly true that a protracted residence on the Western frontier is fatal to the existence of sympathies once cherished for the poor "Indian." The feud between man and the serpent, begun in the Garden of Eden, is not more implacable than that between a frontiersman and a Sioux. Hence, Minnesota will continue without shame or remorse, to pay bounties for Sioux scalps, as other states pay for wolf scalps. It is a "State right" that will not be given up.*
>
> *The operations under the State policy are active, and the papers boast, successful. The correspondence above has this account of the incidents and character of the conflict as now waged under State auspices.*
>
> *"Stray Indian horse thieves are constantly being killed along the frontier. Two Indians were surrounded on the prairie a few days since by twelve*

> *soldiers, and they fought like tigers. One loaded and fired eight times, and the other four; and they did not fall until one was pierced with eight bullets, and the other with six, any one of inflicted a mortal wound. A bullet would pass through their bodies without causing them to flinch. The State scouts, and a large bounty offered to those who chose to hunt independently, is resulting in the 'taking off' of numerous red devils, and will prevent the depopulation of the frontier."*
>
> *A Washington correspondent of the paper from which these extracts are quoted, gave a few days since a very discouraging account of moral and political condition of these western Indians, and advised they be mustered quickly into the United States military service, to keep them out of mischief. Unless the Minnesota hunters are checked in their pastime, there will be few recruits left us when we begin to swear in the red-skins.*

So whose scalp generated the largest bounty in Minnesota? On July 3, 1863, Hutchinson settler Nathan Lampson and his son murdered a Native

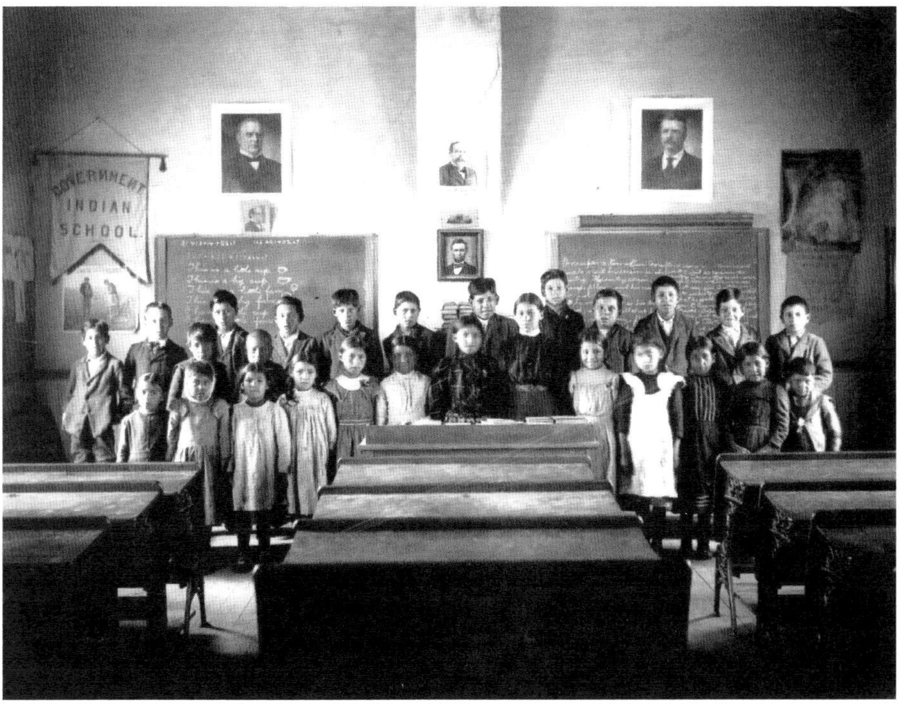

Children attending Government Indian School. Notice that the boys have had their long hair cut off.

American who was gathering berries with his son. The youngster escaped. The scalp for the murdered Indian garnered the usual $25 bounty. But once authorities established that the scalp belonged to Little Crow, the Dakota chief who reluctantly led his tribe in the U.S.-Dakota Conflict of 1862, Lampson was paid an additional $200.

The Minnesota Historical Society received Little Crow's scalp, stretched and cured on a frame, in 1868, and his skull arrived later in 1896. Other bones were added to the collection over the years. In 1971, in an act of goodwill, the remains were returned to his family for a proper burial.

Ironically, scalps of Native Americans continue to be profitable on the black market. As recently as September 2009, the FBI investigated an ad placed on a popular website offering nine preserved scalps from the 1700s for sale in Maine. A federal law enacted in 1990 requires remains to be returned to their native tribes.

This isn't a happy story, but it's one that needs to be told. If not for Chief Wabasha's words, I might still misunderstand the history of scalping.

The Myth of Andrew Volstead

A Trip with Big Carl

Dear Diary,

I recently took a trip to see the Andrew J. Volstead House museum with Big Carl, a mountain of a man who formerly taught cultural anthropology. Carl drove and offered me the daily crossword puzzle, suggesting we could work on it together. He's pretty good at it and was guessing words before I had even given the entire clue. This leads me to two conclusions. Either he's very brilliant, or he did the crossword puzzle earlier that morning and then picked up a fresh newspaper in order to impress me. Either way, neither of us was smart enough to work the New York Times *puzzle. Forget it.*

Our first stop in Granite Falls was on the east end of town for lunch at the Grinder Coffee House. The Grinder not only serves fabulous soup, sandwiches, coffee and dessert, but it also offers a vintage setting with a large window looking out on a granite outcropping with birds, squirrels and an occasional fat cat to watch. It looks good, smells good, sounds good and feels good at the Grinder.

Our next stop was at the brand-new Granite Falls City Hall, where my good friend Bill, the city manager, gave us a tour. Bill and I squeezed Big Carl into Bill's car, and he showed us the flood mitigation work that has been completed on the city in response to two life-changing floods that took place in the last couple of decades.

After that, Carl and I headed to the Andrew J. Volstead House museum, just a few blocks away. Volstead, a well-respected Norwegian lawyer, held

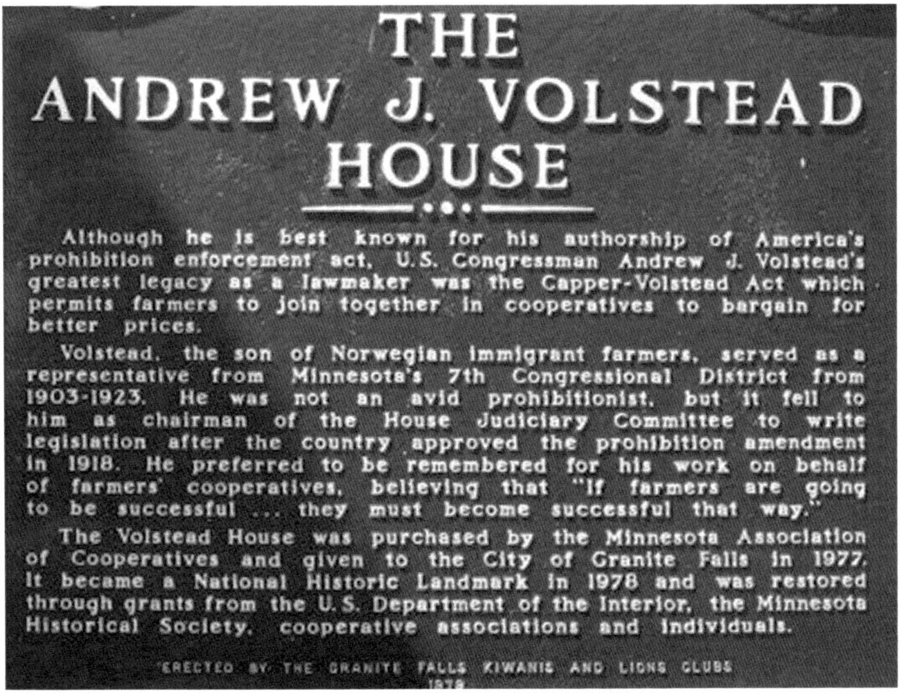

Marker outside of the historic Andrew Volstead House in Granite Falls, Minnesota.

several local offices in Minnesota before serving (1903–23) in the U.S. House of Representatives, and chaired the Judiciary Committee, which oversaw passage of the Volstead Act, the Eighteenth Amendment to the Constitution, establishing the practice of Prohibition.

We headed down into the Minnesota River Valley, following the Minnesota River National Scenic Byway to the Joseph R. Brown memorial in order for me to take a couple of photographs. It's the strangest thing. We got lost on the way and ended up taking a more scenic route than planned.

We managed to locate the foundation that marks the twelve-room house Brown had built for his family and that suffered extensive damage during the U.S.-Dakota Conflict of 1862, and I snapped a couple of shots. And then, on the way back to Highway 212, we got lost again. I don't see how that is even possible, but it happened. My excuse is that I was trying to figure out that damnable New York Times *crossword puzzle.*

I can't be expected to do everything.

—Minnesota Country Mouse

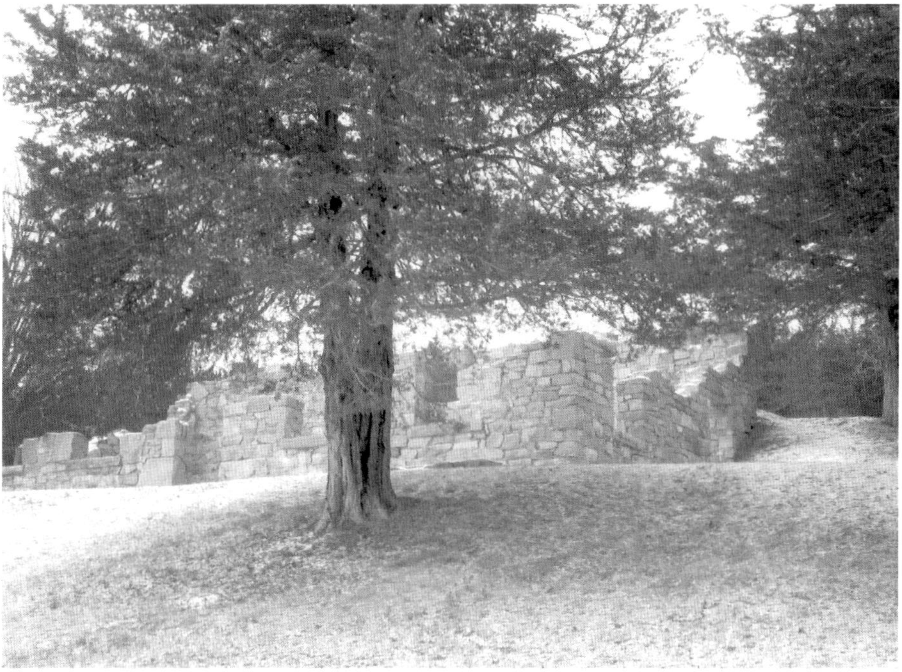

Joseph R. Brown Memorial located along the Minnesota River Valley Scenic Byway between Belview and Sacred Heart, Minnesota.

A charming and beautifully preserved clapboard house, built in 1878, now serves with distinction as a museum in a quiet southwestern Minnesota River town. It stands at 163 Ninth Street in Granite Falls, where, several blocks to the east, the Minnesota River slips quietly past the downtown business district. This vintage building was home to Congressman Andrew J. Volstead from 1894 to 1930.

As a rule, most U.S. citizens probably will not recognize the congressman's name. But for those who lived in the early part of the twentieth century, the name Volstead defines a thirteen-year era of upheaval, black markets, prostitution, gangsters and stills. Volstead, a well-respected Norwegian lawyer, chaired the judiciary committee that oversaw passage of the Volstead Act, the Eighteenth Amendment to the Constitution establishing Prohibition.

The signing of the bill was the fruit of the nationwide Temperance movement, a crusade inspired by evangelical Christians and the "respectable classes." Middle-class citizens eventually joined the cause, endorsing "moral suasion" to convince Congress that the production and sale of alcohol should be made illegal in the United States. Prohibition on alcohol lasted from 1920

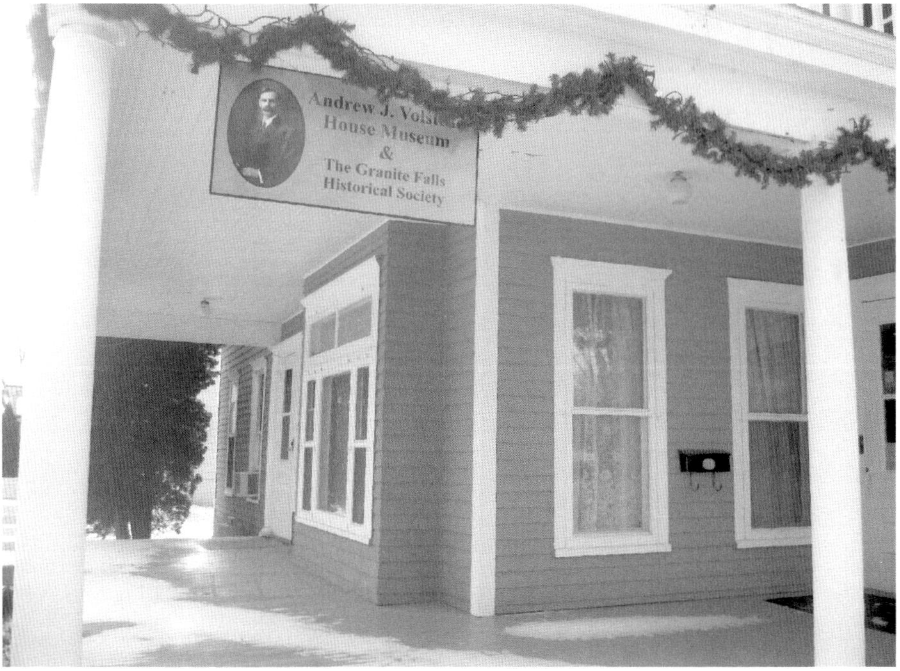

The historic Andrew Volstead House in Granite Falls, Minnesota.

to 1933 and has been filed away in history as "the thirteen-year failure," a testament to the notion that government cannot legislate morality.

A surprising proponent of prohibition was Yale economist Irving Fischer, whose fellow eugenicists believed that removing alcohol from public consumption would invigorate the population and help create a super-race of men and women, as well as guarantee a 20 percent rise in industrial productivity. The group also believed that a system of arranged marriages between men of distinction and women of wealth would create a gifted race.

The congressman's name on this bill led many to believe that Volstead was a crusader for morality. But he was not a reformer. Rather, Volstead was a well-respected, hardworking citizen with many friends who, except during Prohibition, enjoyed an occasional cocktail.

Despite his detachment from the National Prohibition Act, Volstead became inextricably tied to the Eighteenth Amendment by the public. For thirteen years they cried, "Up with Volstead!" or, "Down with Volstead!" depending upon which side of the argument they stood.

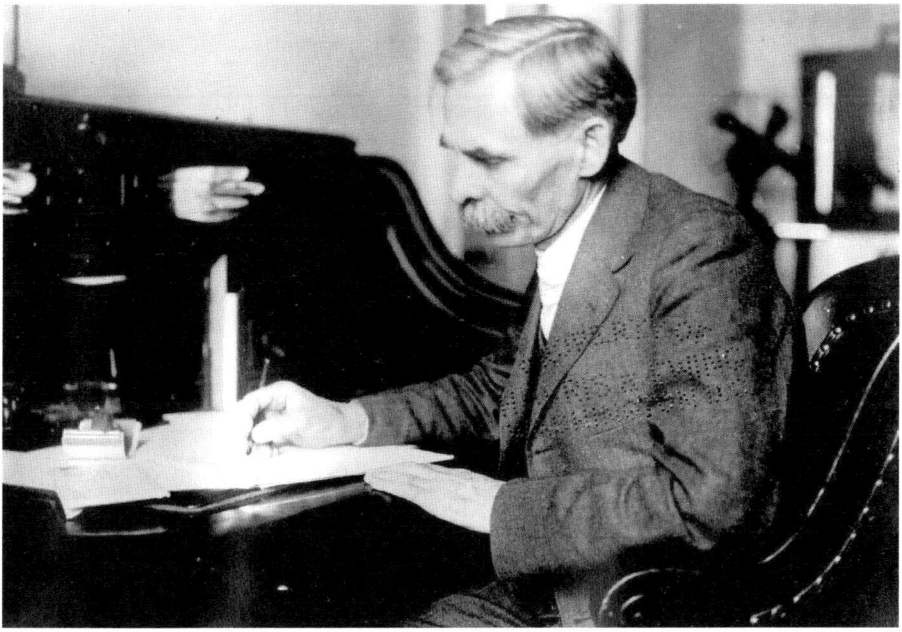

Andrew Volstead working at his desk. *Courtesy of Terri Dinneson, Granite Falls Historical Society, Granite Falls, Minnesota.*

The community of Granite Falls is very proud of Volstead but downplays his connection to Prohibition. Instead, this river town highlights the Capper-Volstead Act, signed into law on February 18, 1922, by President Warren Harding. Referred to as the Magna Carta of cooperatives in the agricultural industry, the Capper-Volstead Act allows farmers to work to collectively market their produce. Under earlier antitrust laws, those collaborative actions may otherwise have been prohibited. The original antitrust legislation came from the practice of huge trusts on the East Coast buying up all producers of a single commodity, which then removed all competition. The huge trusts could then set whatever price they wanted for steel and other products.

The Capper-Volstead Act is specific to farmers, enabling them to join together to not only negotiate fair prices but also share the risks that come with a late harvest and other farm-related risk factors. The act is specific to the production of the crop and not the processing of the product.

Bootlegging Tales

Bootleggers

Dear Journal,

Bootleggers Supper Club, an old roadhouse on the edge of Granite Falls, Minnesota, was doing a bang-up business Friday night when Cindy and Bill and I arrived. We were lucky and got a table with a good view of singer and songwriter Jerry Ostensoe and quirky bass player Richard Handeen. (In my world, quirky is a very good thing, indeed.)

The food is always good, but it's the popovers with honey butter that Cindy looks forward to, and we got them. We were having a good time, kind of bobbing our heads to the music, when this incredibly attractive dark-haired family walked in, and I could feel the vibration in the dining room pick up. It was the bass player's daughter, Malena, toting an accordion of sorts. Well, she got set up with the group and rounded out the music, making the food take a back seat to the entertainment.

"Wow, she's gorgeous," Bill said, referring to Malena, not the accordion. Yup, we all smiled, and agreed she is that. "I didn't even know I liked accordion music before." Sure, sure. Cindy and I nodded. "She can really play," Bill continued. Cindy just rolled her eyes. Lucky Bill, his birthday is coming up soon and now that I see how much he enjoys accordion music, I know what to get him! He's getting the Best of the Six Fat Dutchmen CD.

—Minnesota Country Mouse

On the western edge of Granite Falls, beyond the family neighborhoods, isolated by trees, fields and sloughs, Bootlegger's Supper Club stands as a reminder of Granite Falls' connection to Prohibition. The restaurant boasts "made from scratch food that's so good it should be illegal."

The supper club, an old speakeasy formerly known as Skunk Hollow, was moved here in 1949 from a heavily wooded site along the Minnesota River near Wegdahl. Today, local musicians provide homegrown music here, and once in a while, Brau Brothers Brewing Company, a small brewery from nearby Lucan, hosts beer-tasting nights.

The building has a colorful history. An old-timer, now deceased, regaled Bootlegger's owner with Prohibition-era tales suggesting that Prohibition was a running joke with drinkers. It seemed to him that only federal agents took the law seriously. He recalled those agents unwisely driving enormous yellow Packards that could be seen for miles cruising along the flat prairie roads on their way to break up a party or a still.

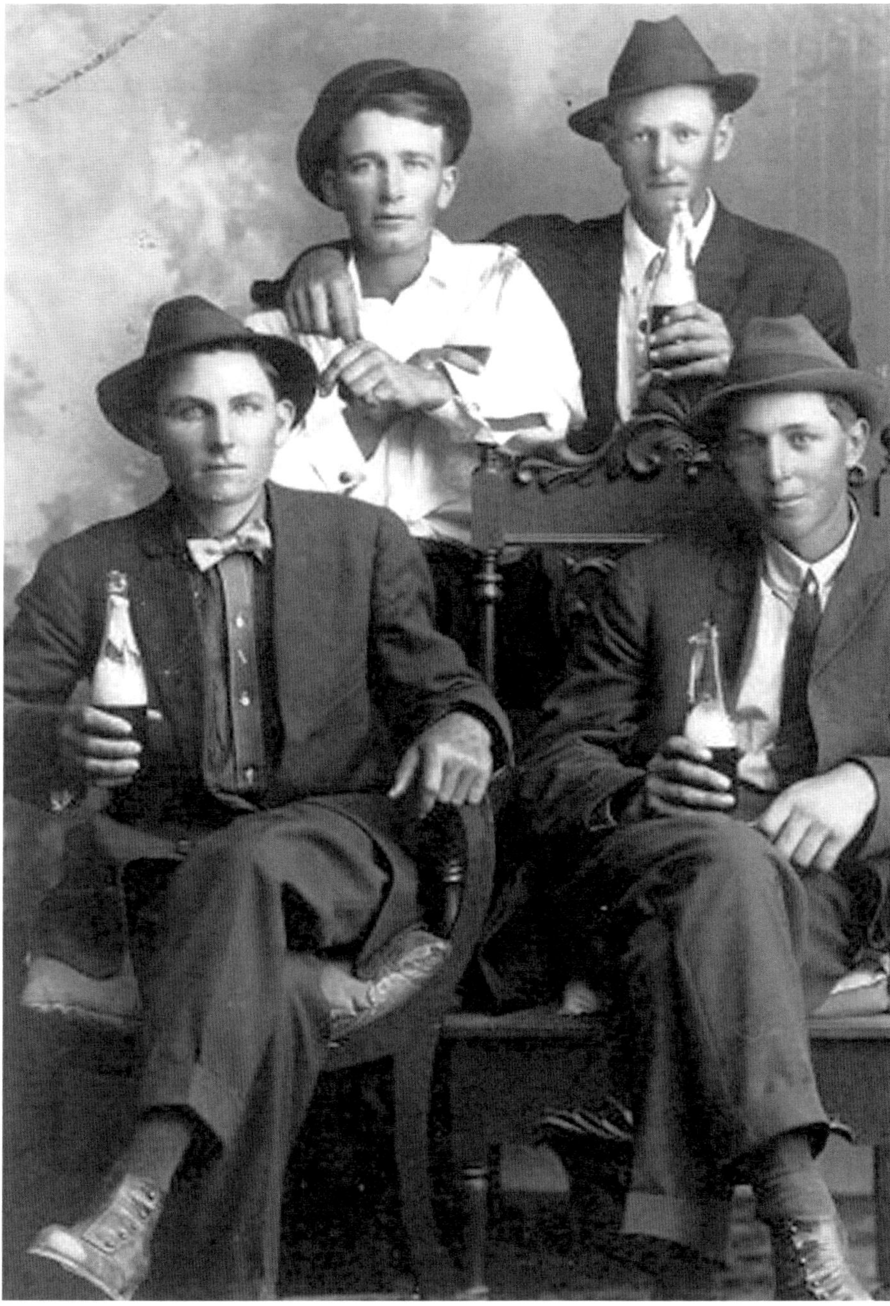

Antique postcard of men enjoying drinks, from the Angie Bergen Collection. *Courtesy of Monica Fischer, Wabasso, Minnesota.*

My old dad throws his head back and laughs out loud when he tells the story of his much older sister, Elvera, who attended a dance in the 1920s. A deeply concerned gentleman approached Elvera and warned her that she had been talking to a bootlegger.

"Well," she told him, "he's my cousin!"

Discovering the Softer Side of J. Edgar Hoover

I was talking to my childhood friend Cindy, and making arrangements to visit Granite Falls in the central section of the Minnesota River Valley, when she remarked about a collection of letters from J. Edgar Hoover at the city offices. I assumed she was mistaken and probably mixed this notorious figure up with someone else.

"Are you sure?" I asked Cindy. But her husband, Bill, the city manager, confirmed the existence of the Hoover letters.

You could have knocked me over with a feather. It just didn't make any sense. It turned out Hoover wrote the letters to Laura Volstead Lomen, daughter of Congressman Andrew J. Volstead, a well-respected lawyer from Granite Falls who was elected to the U.S. House of Representatives in 1902, and they were discovered in a brown paper bag in a the drawer of a desk at the Andrew J. Volstead House.

Cindy wasn't sure what their relationship entailed, but a visit to the Andrew J. Volstead House museum laid the mystery to rest. Lomen and Hoover met while attending college at George Washington University in Washington, D.C.

Why should I be astonished at this unlikely relationship? Well, because we're talking about the powerful mastermind behind the Federal Bureau of Investigation and father of modern law enforcement in the United States. President Calvin Coolidge appointed Hoover as the FBI's first director in 1924, marking the beginning of a career that spanned eight presidential administrations through nearly fifty years.

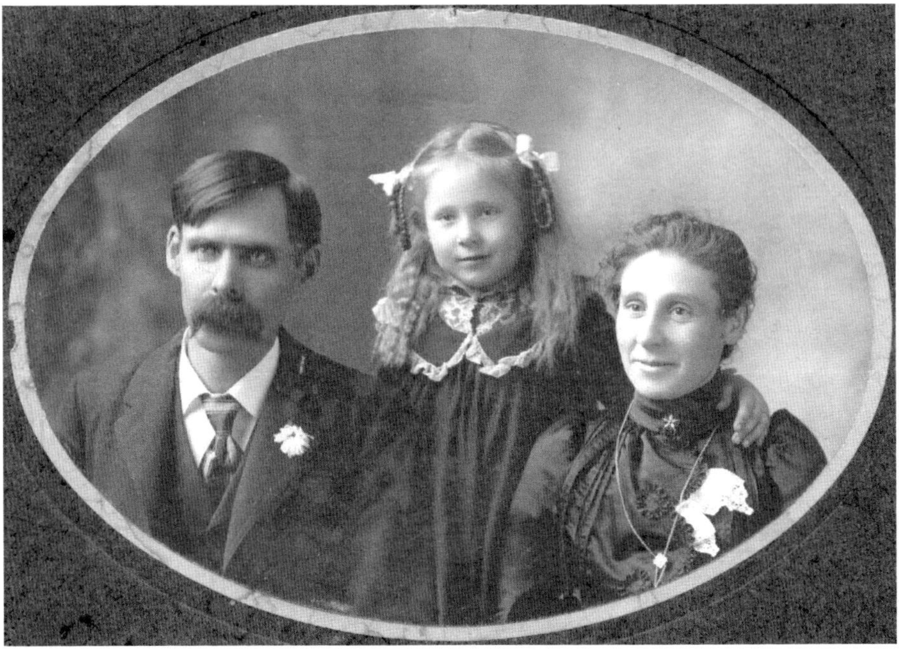

Laura Volstead as a child in a family photograph. *Courtesy of Terri Dinneson, Granite Falls Historical Society, Granite Falls, Minnesota.*

Hoover is one of the most controversial figures in the history and scandal of U.S. politics. Hoover's biographies are filled with mention of his racism, blackmail and nebulous sexual orientation. Decades of collecting files on celebrities, politicians and individuals he pegged subversive, as well as the occasional gangster, made Hoover a problem for the government. He was a man to be reckoned with.

DELIGHTFUL SENSE OF HUMOR

My research into the colorful life of Hoover, however, did not prepare me for the letters he wrote to his friend Laura. I saw, in his writing, a man capable of being a friend. He shows tenderness and compassion and, on occasion, a delightful sense of humor. For instance, a July 10, 1957 letter addressed to Laura begins: "Dear Laura, It is not necessary for me to have fingerprints in order to recognize a friend of this Bureau."

JOHN EDGAR HOOVER
DIRECTOR

Federal Bureau of Investigation
United States Department of Justice
Washington, D. C.

April 22, 1958

Dear Laura:

Thanks very much for your letter of April 15. It was good to hear from you again and to learn that Carl is able to enjoy a bit of the outdoors. I am sure this is doing him a world of good.

Naturally, I was very pleased to receive your kind comments concerning my recent book and also my receipt of the President's Award for Distinguished Federal Civilian Service. This was an honor which I felt was shared by all the employees of this Bureau, and we were all grateful for such recognition. In accordance with your request I am happy to forward, under separate cover, a copy of the picture taken at the time of the presentation.

You were fortunate in having such a mild winter for it seems like most of the country suffered from one of the severest winters in years. I know Washington experienced more cold weather and snow than we have seen in some time, and it is good to see the flowers and the green grass once again.

Do let me hear from you again, and with my kindest regards and best wishes to you and Carl, I am

Sincerely,

Edgar

Letter from J. Edgar Hoover to Congressman Andrew Volstead's daughter. *Courtesy of Bill Lavin and the Granite Falls City Office and Historical Society, Granite Falls, Minnesota.*

In another letter, dated December 12, 1967, Hoover writes, "I spied your name in the article concerning the dedication of the museum at Granite Falls and was pleased with the recognition given you. I am sure you enjoyed the ceremonies, especially since you saw so many of your old friends. The two museums must be very pleased to have the material of your father's that you located, as they must consider them valuable additions to their collections."

In his letters, Hoover occasionally refers to current events. On March 8, 1957, he writes, "The current investigation of labor racketeering is causing quite a stir here also and of course we have considerable interest in it. I only hope this is not another means of securing publicity with no action or benefits resulting therefrom."

In the labor racketeering case, although the Senate McClellan Committee began making labor racketeering a national issue in the 1950s, it wasn't until two decades later, after Hoover's death, that the FBI began making organized crime control a priority.

In April 1958, Hoover thanks Laura for her kind comments regarding his newly published book, *Masters of Deceit: The Story of Communism in America and How to Fight It*. He also offers his appreciation for her recognition of the President's Award for Distinguished Federal Civilian Service that he received.

A letter sent on June 10, 1968, mentions a wire Laura sent congratulating him in regard to the James Earl Ray case. (Ray confessed to the assassination of civil rights leader Martin Luther King on April 4, 1968, and was sentenced to ninety-nine years in prison. He later recanted his confession.) Hoover also thanks her for newspaper clippings in 1966 "pertaining to the assassination and Warren Commission Report."

The box full of letters spans thirty years, thanking Laura for birthday, Easter and Christmas greetings. Hoover's notes sometimes mention tidbits of his personal life: "The sockeye salmon arrived today and you can be sure that I will follow the instructions included in your letter of September 21, in order to get the best results."

Hoover kindly sent condolences to Laura when her husband, Carl, died. On the occasion of her father's death, Hoover writes: "You certainly can have consolation in the thought that he led a full and active life, having the confidence and good will of his fellow man."

Their friendship lasted for decades, and the letters show an unexpectedly gentle and poetic side of the man who kept detailed dossiers on his enemies and his friends.

"Dear Laura, It is typically thoughtful of you to remember my birthday—many, many thanks for your wire and your card, which arrived for the occasion. Hearing from friends is always the most heartwarming part of such a celebration, and I did want you to know how much I appreciate your kind thought of me. It helped make the day a very happy one indeed. With best wishes for 1967, Sincerely, Edgar."

Cut Nose, the Skeleton in Dr. Mayo's Closet

The locals called him "Little Doctor Mayo," referring to his short stature. But the five-foot, four-inch Dr. William Worrall Mayo was anything but short in importance. Early settlers along the southeastern end of the Minnesota River Valley respected this doctor who wore a top hat and tails and carried his medical instruments in his pockets, apparently unconcerned with sepsis.

The well-educated Mayo—he had studied medicine at Indiana Medical College and practiced pharmacy at Bellevue Hospital in Manhattan, New York—worked not only as a physician but also as a pharmacist, horse doctor and ferryman on the Minnesota River. He juggled the jobs to support his wife and sons. The Mayos had moved to the area in 1856 and three years later built a house in Le Sueur. Later, Mayo and his sons would go on to found the world-renowned Mayo Clinic in Rochester, Minnesota.

As luck would have it, the Civil War worked in Mayo's favor, providing him with a regular flow of patients needing medical exams to enter the army. During the U.S.-Dakota Conflict of 1862, Mayo treated the wounded in New Ulm, a town at the center of the conflict between settlers and Native Americans.

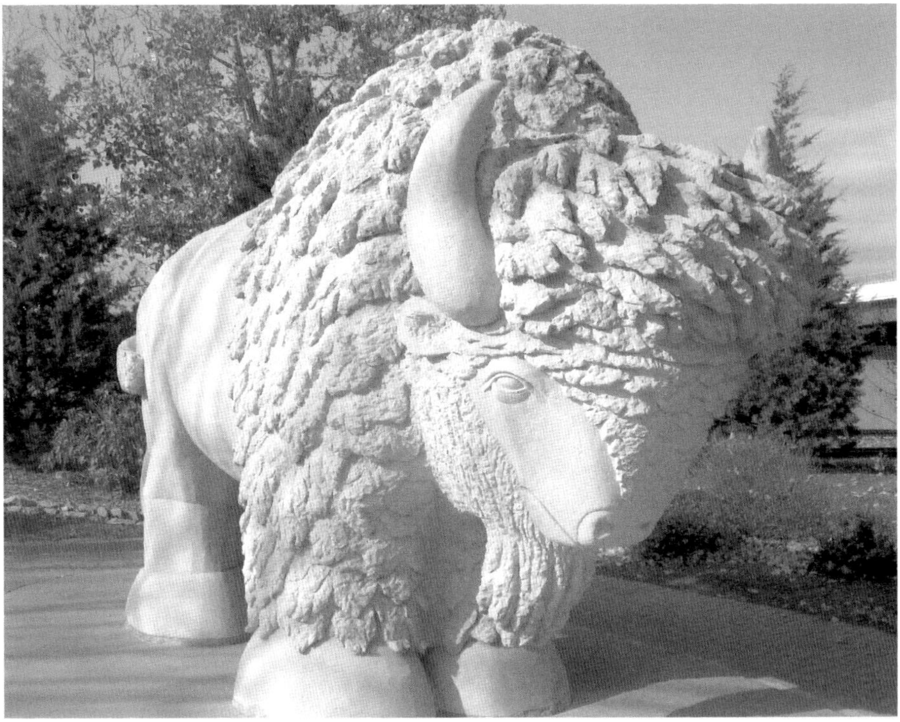

Statue at Reconciliation Park marking the place where thirty-eight Native Americans were executed, after the U.S.-Dakota Conflict of 1862, in the largest mass execution in our country's history. Mankato, Minnesota.

LARGEST MASS EXECUTION IN U.S. HISTORY

After the Dakota were defeated in the late summer conflict of 1862, President Abraham Lincoln, who already had his hands full with the Civil War, sentenced thirty-eight Dakota to death. A gallows large enough to accommodate all thirty-eight was built along the shore of the Minnesota River. On December 26, 1862, thousands of soldiers and citizens gathered in Mankato, Minnesota, to view the execution, the largest mass hanging in U.S. history. The bodies were removed and buried in a shallow, frozen grave along the sandy bank of the river.

Among those hanged was Cut Nose, a member of the Lower Sioux Mdewakanton tribe, a warrior and the alleged leader of the New Ulm Massacre. His given name was *Marpiya Okinajin*, meaning "He Who Stands in Clouds."

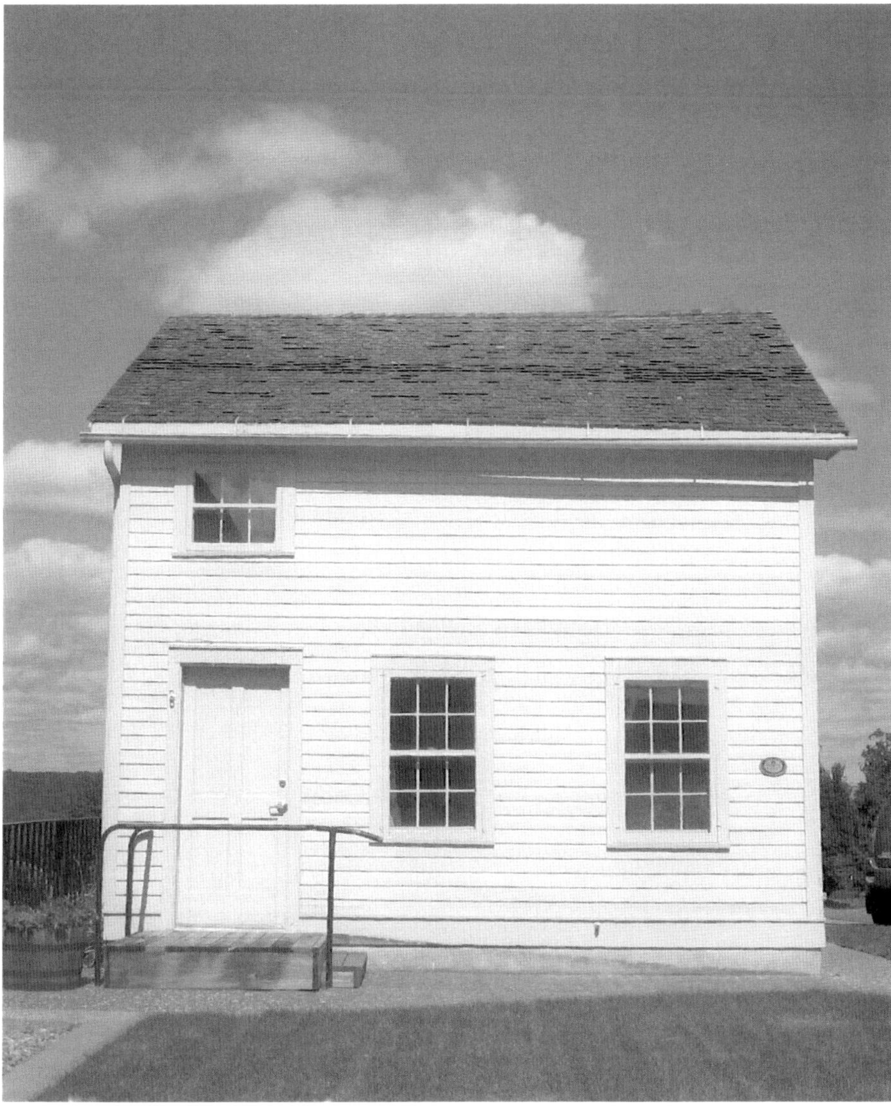

The Frederick Kiesling House in New Ulm, Minnesota, was one of three houses in that community surviving the U.S.-Dakota Conflict of 1862.

Grave Robbing

On the evening of December 26, Mayo led a cadre of doctors to the mass grave site. There he bribed the lone guard, convincing him to help dig up the very grave he was guarding. The doctors stole away with several wagons full of bodies, losing only one of the thirty-eight as they climbed the steep riverbank, drove through the deserted streets of Mankato and headed to a barn near St. Peter. There they lay the bodies out for proper freezing in preparation for selling their macabre commodity, shipping them as far away as Chicago, Illinois.

From the lot, Mayo chose the corpse of Cut Nose, identifiable by a facial deformity. He and his fellow doctors later dissected the body at Mayo's residence and studied it for educational purposes. In the interest of commerce, Cut Nose's skin was removed for tanning, trimming, tattooing and selling as souvenirs in Mankato.

Mayo dismembered Cut Nose's body, boiled and articulated the bones and then kept the remains in a large kettle in his office. Some people said he used the bones to help his patients understand their own injuries better, but members of the tribe say he kept the kettle full of bones in his office out of spite, or for bragging rights.

His children were allowed to play with the bones, and one of his sons, at the age of four, would try and put the skeleton together like a puzzle, occasionally being corrected by his father. It would be hard to deny the value of learning about the human body from such an exercise.

WHERE IS CUT NOSE'S SKELETON?

The skeleton was varnished and reassembled and hung in the Mayo Clinic for years. In July 2000, a piece of Cut Nose's skin was returned to the Lower Sioux Community near Morton, from a museum in Michigan, after an inventory mandated by the Native American Graves Protection and Repatriation Act of 1998.

After much probing by the Native American community, Cut Nose's skull was finally returned by the Mayo Clinic, but what about his skeleton? A former Mayo Clinic employee who returned a kneecap to the tribe in 2009 is confident that the bones lie in a box on a shelf somewhere in the bowels of the clinic. Or maybe, could it be, that Cut Nose's skeleton is still hanging in the back of Dr. William Worrall Mayo's closet?

August Schell Brewing Company

Heritage

Dear Diary,

Melanie and I visited New Ulm earlier this year and didn't get around to doing or seeing nearly everything we wanted. We stopped at an antique store located in this wonderful building with two spiral staircases. Melanie doesn't know it, but the house next door also had antiques in it. I didn't say anything, or we would never have gotten out of there.

If there is one thing you can say about New Ulm, Minnesota, they do not have an identity crisis. They know exactly who they are with their colorful German heritage. There are a variety of cultural events and activities each year.

We saw some guys driving a team of horses hitched to an old-fashioned beer wagon on the road leading out of the Schell's Brewery. The gardens this year are the most beautiful I've ever seen them, and it was the first time I had seen their restaurant (or was it a pub?) overlooking the valley. I've never taken the tour to see how they brew beer there. I guess that's something else to put on our list of things to do.

—Minnesota Country Mouse

The 150-year-old August Schell Brewing Company, located on the edge of New Ulm in southwestern Minnesota, is like a tiny slice of heaven in an area known more for its constant wind and wide-open spaces than for

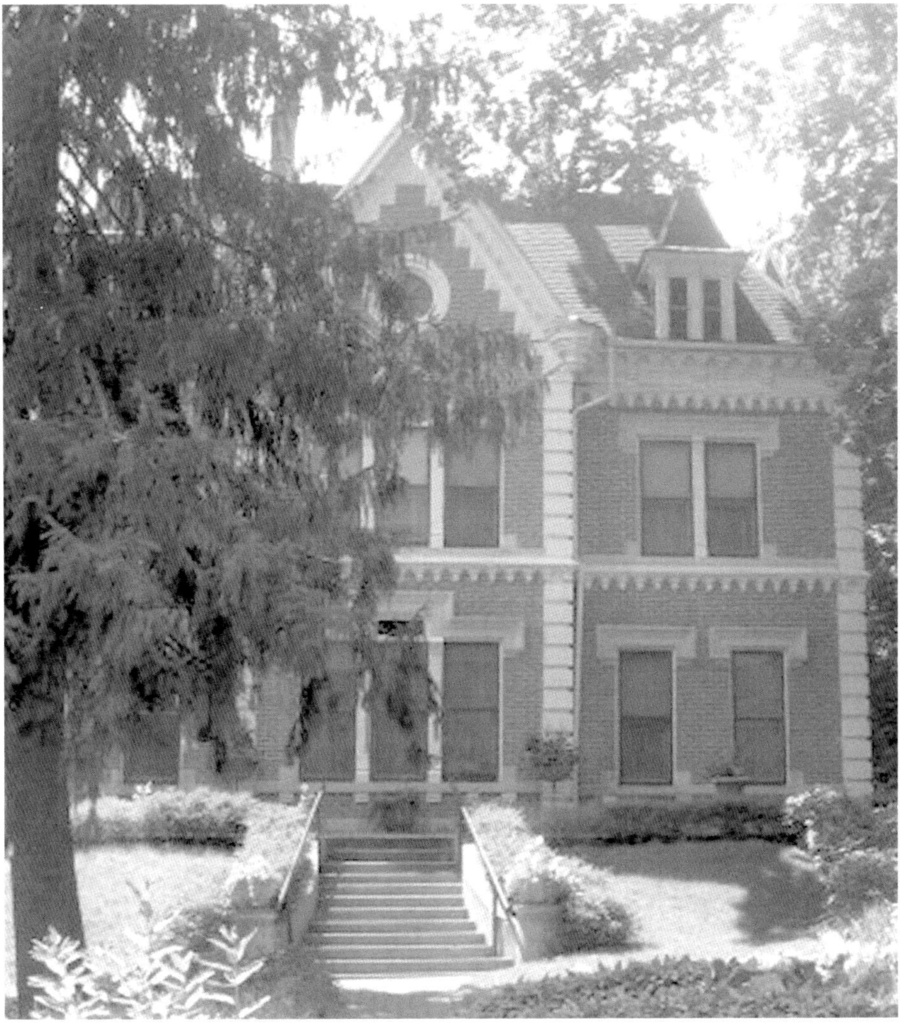

The mansion on the August Schell Brewery property in New Ulm, Minnesota.

its charm. I'm sure I've seen pixies and gnomes among the foliage in the gardens surrounding the brewery.

August Schell Brewing Company is Old World Germany tucked snugly into a wooded ravine near an artesian spring along the Cottonwood River. The brewery is surrounded by hills overflowing with fauna and flora. Vines, heavy with hops, hang from an arbor near the brewery.

Built in 1860, the Schell's Brewery is the second oldest family-owned brewery in the state. The first brewery in Minnesota was the Yoerg Brewing

Company established in 1848, the year its founder, Anthony Yoerg, migrated from Bavaria to St. Paul, Minnesota. Yoerg Brewing closed in 1952.

Schell's has its beginnings in Germany, where, during the March Revolution of 1848, thousands of nationalists across Europe joined to demand freedom of the press and freedom of assembly and were met with violence and terror. A large number of Europeans, many of whom were soldiers and politicians, migrated to America in 1848. These immigrants became known as the Forty-Eighters.

Among them was twenty-year-old August Schell from Durbach, located in the heart of the Black Forest region of Germany, who landed in New Orleans. Trained as a machinist, he worked his way up the Mississippi and Ohio Rivers, settling in Cincinnati. About 1853, he met and married Theresa Hermann and quickly added two baby girls to the family.

They met other German immigrants belonging to a group known as the Cincinnati Turners, who promoted nationalist gymnastics. The Cincinnati Turners, as a political group, supported the election of Abraham Lincoln and also provided the bodyguard at his inauguration.

Schell, his wife, Theresa, and their two small daughters traveled with the Cincinnati Turners to the Minnesota River Valley, where they had heard

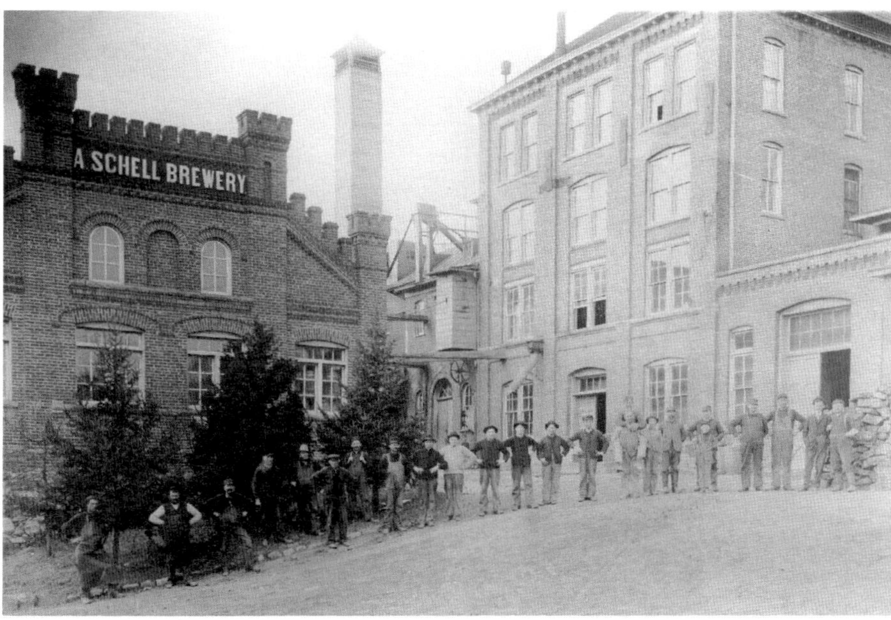

Workers at the August Schell Brewing Company. *Courtesy of the Schell Brewing Company, New Ulm, Minnesota.*

a German settlement was struggling to survive. They joined the settlers and, finding strength in numbers, banded together to found the captivating community of New Ulm.

It didn't take long for Schell to realize that good German beer was hard to come by in this new settlement. So he started a brewery, teaming up with Jacob Bernardt, a brewmaster from the Benzberg Brewery in St. Paul. That brewery, after a brief existence, was incorporated into the Minnesota Brewing Company.

Bavarian immigrant and brewmaster Jacob Schmidt also worked with Schell. Schmidt had traveled the Midwest, offering his expertise to a variety of breweries, including the Hamm's Brewery established in St. Paul in 1865 by Theodore Hamm. Schmidt eventually purchased a half-share in the Northstar Brewing Company in 1884 and later named it the Jacob Schmidt Brewing Company.

The bucolic Schell's Brewery setting with its woods and springs, though legally occupied by the Schell family in the eyes of the burgeoning government, was not completely theirs. The indigenous people who had been forced from the location shortly before its purchase were now starving on small tracts of land along the Minnesota River.

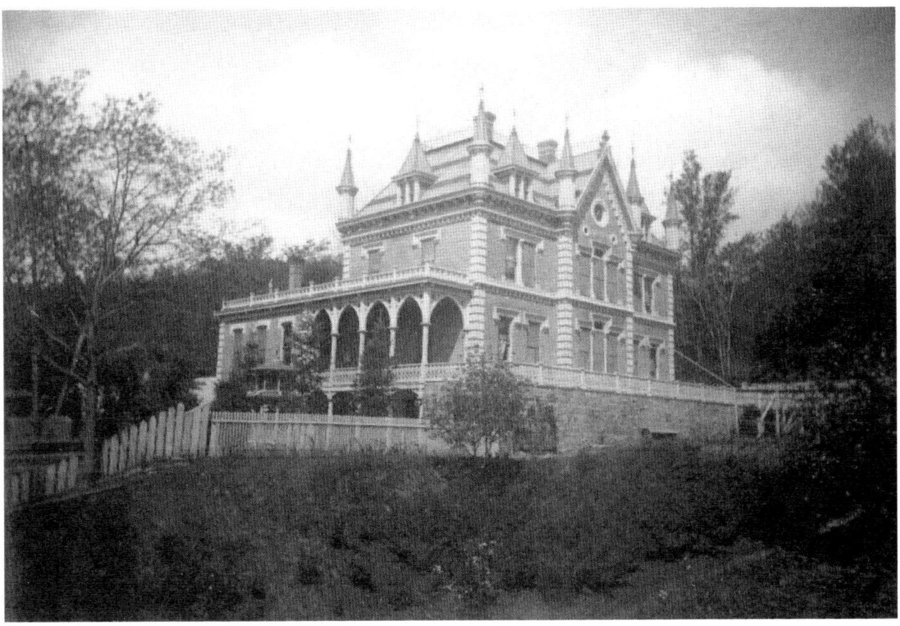

The Schell Mansion. *Courtesy of the Schell Brewing Company, New Ulm, Minnesota.*

The Schell family was not blind to the suffering of the Native Americans and helped them when they were able by providing them with food. Perhaps their own oppression, at the hands of the cruel government they left behind in Germany, had left an indelible mark on their souls. It is believed by the Schell descendants that August and Theresa's innate goodness helped preserve the brewery during the U.S.-Dakota Conflict of 1862, which wiped out much of the New Ulm settlement.

Another example of August Schell's sense of fairness was proven in 1866 when his partner, Jacob Bernhardt, became ill and decided to sell his share of the brewery. Schell made the generous choice to put the entire brewery up for sale in order to maximize his ailing partner's profit. Schell's own bid for $12,000 was the highest, and he and Theresa became sole owners of the brewery.

The Schells worked hard and lived right, watching their family grow from two children to six. In 1885, they built the stately Schell Mansion.

Prohibition

A movement began growing in the 1880s toward the prohibition of alcohol in the United States. It picked up steam in the early 1900s, and by 1919, Minnesota senator Andrew Volstead from Granite Falls, about one hundred miles up the Minnesota River from New Ulm, was poised, with pen in hand, to sign the Eighteenth Amendment. This amendment, known as the Volstead Act, made the production and possession of liquor illegal across the country.

Breweries met the challenge by securing licenses to brew a "near beer" with a low alcohol content deemed acceptable by the federal government. During Prohibition, the August Schell Brewery was accused of teetering over that line. Members of the Schell family found themselves in St. Paul defending their brew to federal authorities. Lengthy storage of the product, they explained, had caused the alcohol content to rise. The feds saw this as a reasonable explanation, and the brewery escaped indictment.

The Schells kept their brewery operating through thirteen years of Prohibition by diversifying their products and by selling candy and soft drinks in addition to near beer.

Small Breweries Challenged by Cans

Peter Durand of England secured a patent from King George III in 1810 for the very first tin can. In 1933, the American Can Company developed a lining for its cans to prevent the metal from reacting with the beer. The company called it vinylite and trademarked it Keglined. These developments changed the beer industry dramatically, threatening Schell's existence.

Before the creation of the tin can, breweries catered to their own small regions, delivering their products in returnable bottles and kegs. Beer cans made it possible for one-way shipping, increasing the size of the territory a company could serve. Breweries on the edge of technology could claim their market share with great advantage, leaving those still selling their products in bottles behind.

Long after beer was sold in cans, my old dad still purchased his Schell's in heavy cardboard cases holding two dozen amber bottles. Every couple of months, we kids, happy to take a trip off the farm, waited in the old green station wagon for him to return the case of empty bottles to the local bar and come back out with a full one. Later, back home, I would sip the foam (when it was my turn) off the top of my old dad's freshly opened Schell's beer bottle. Dad wasn't much of a drinker. He said any more than three beers gave him a headache. I noticed they also made his forehead shiny and his laugh a little louder.

With the advent of World War II, metal was needed for artillery, not beer, and the threat of being overtaken by a new means of distribution stalled briefly.

By the time the aluminum can was introduced in 1958, the Schell Brewery was struggling. Small breweries were quickly being purchased and consolidated with larger ones. Faced with financial challenges, the Schell family sold an enormous walnut tree imported from Germany as a seedling when Schell was diversifying by planting wine grapes and trees.

With luck and good planning, August Schell Brewery conquered the challenges presented by new technology. It returned to its roots, brewing award-winning craft beers, and is thriving today, a true asset to the German community of New Ulm.

If you were to visit the brewery today, you would find peacocks strolling around the beautiful grounds that include gardens, a fountain and a deer garden. That's right. Deer, not beer. In fact, the Schell's logo is a deer with imposing antlers. Visitors can also tour a free museum, a tavern and a gift shop at this family-friendly place. Brewery tours are available for a small charge.

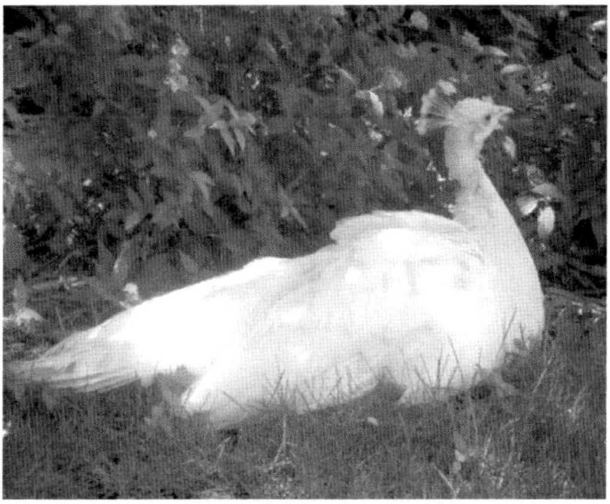

Albino peacock at the August Schell Brewing Company gardens in New Ulm, Minnesota.

My friend Melanie and I decided to visit the brewery one autumn day when we were tooling around in her hybrid car. We followed the winding lane into the woods and parked alongside the road. Our spirits were fairly bursting with joy at the ripe, grainy scent of a sunburned autumn day. We walked past the old-fashioned buildings, across the brook and into the gardens. I would have been perfectly content to stroll around the grounds taking snapshots of flowers and yakking away to Melanie about how lovely it all is, but then I saw a wedding party. The Schell's gardens are the perfect setting for an outdoor celebration.

That day, the young men in the wedding party wore suits and hats and the bridesmaids were dressed in fluorescent orange and red satin dresses. When the bride lifted the hem of her wedding dress to step up a stairway, we saw, to our delight, that she wore bright red shoes under her snowy gown.

The wedding party gathered on the steps in front of the Schell Mansion for their photo shoot, and I got as close as I could to take pictures. I didn't know the wedding party, but they were simply too striking to ignore. Meanwhile, the real photographer, who was getting paid to take their pictures, looked at me while he wrestled with his equipment and said, "Excuse me!"

I was rightly chastened, shoved my camera back into my lumpy purse and slunk away to sulk. These things happen.

The Historic Olof Swensson Farm

Orb

Dear Diary,

This is going to be fun, because you see, I went back to visit Historic Chippewa City in Montevideo at the eastern end of the Minnesota River with my best friend Cindy, who said she loves history but refused to enter the building with the horse-drawn antique hearse.

"There's a spirit in there," she said, "and if you take a picture of the casket, you're going to see an orb." Some people think orbs are little bits of energy left behind by an individual after their death.

Cindy has a flair for the dramatic, but she was true to her word and wouldn't come near the hearse. I was delighted and surprised that she was right about the orb. You can see one floating in the upper left-hand corner of the photo. It's a faint, little bubble-like apparition. So, I guess she was right—and she won't know it until she reads this post.

I do have a bit of a dark side. It's nothing serious, and I certainly don't spend much time contemplating death, but I know my version of dying is a little different from a lot of folks'. I guess I don't think it's the worst thing that could happen to you. And although I'm afraid of the process, I think once you cross over there's a big party in your honor—on both sides.

There are people I've lost who I'd love to see again. And every year there are more of them. But I'm not in a hurry to go. In fact, I believe I'd better get going and get a bigger kick out of living on this side before my time is

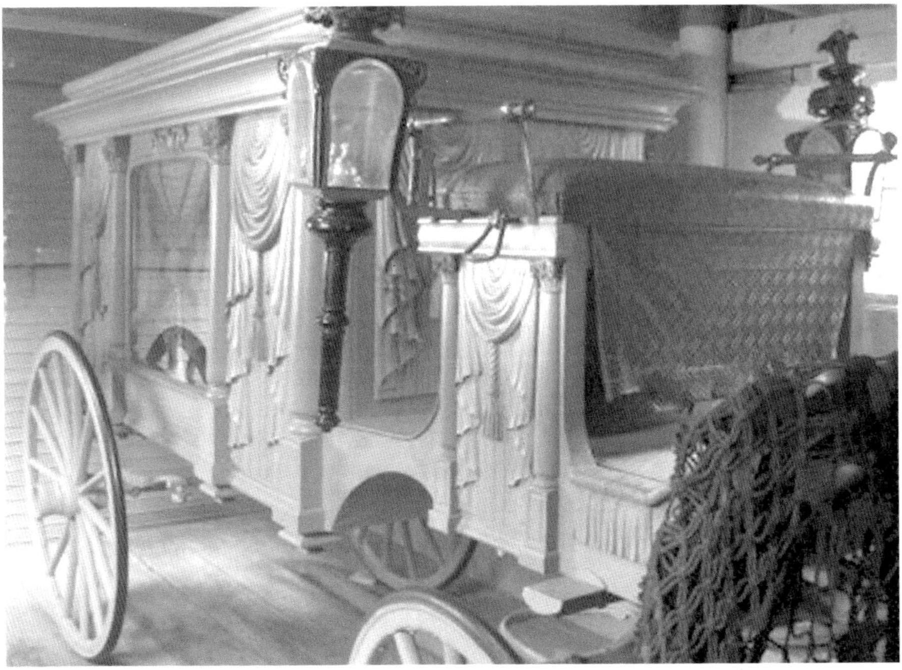

Antique horse-drawn hearse at the Historic Chippewa Village in Montevideo, Minnesota.

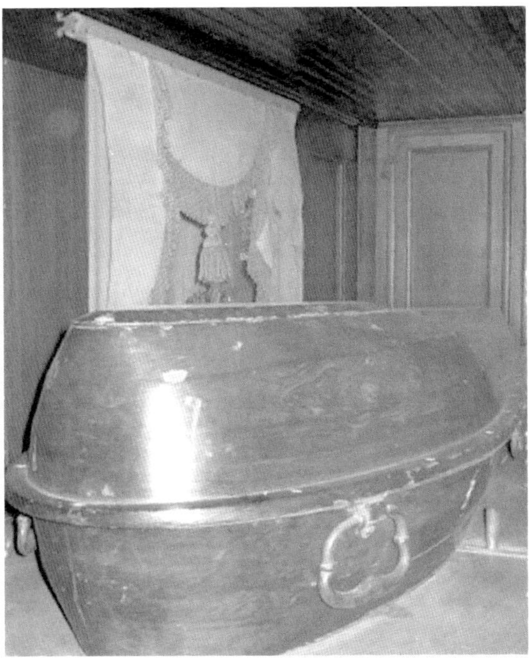

Antique casket at the Historic Chippewa Village in Montevideo, Minnesota.

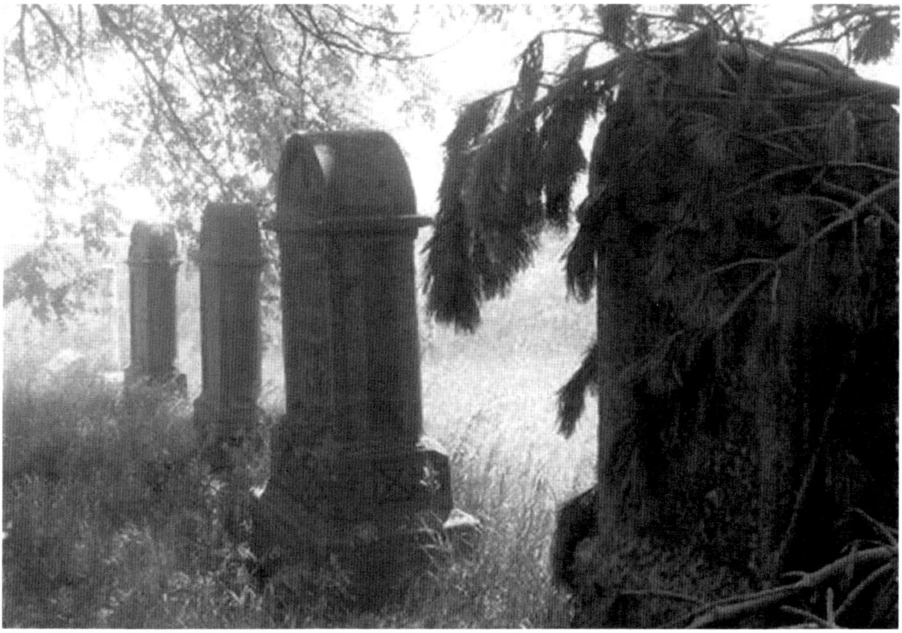

Row of headstones in the family cemetery at the Historic Olof Swensson Farm near Montevideo, Minnesota.

> *up. I'm just better at working than playing. Living life and having fun takes effort, and I've been a little lax in that department, but I'm willing to take it up a notch.*
> *—Minnesota Country Mouse*

My friend Cindy and I decided to give ourselves a little tour of the Historic Olof Swensson Farm between Granite Falls and Montevideo in southwestern Minnesota. Once again, my friend Cindy predicted an orb if I took a picture, this time of the porch at the Historic Olof Swensson Farm in Chippewa County, Minnesota, and once again, an orb showed up on my photo. Cindy wouldn't come anywhere near the porch and worried when I disappeared behind a bush while photographing this turn-of-the-century, twenty-two-room home.

The home was built by immigrant Olof Swensson, who was born May 19, 1843, in Ostmarken, Kongvigers Parish, in Norway. It was designed by Swensson in an Italianate-Georgian style and built in 1901.

Cindy and I have been enjoying the delicious terror of the supernatural since we were in junior high and tried to get Anne Frank to talk to us through

Cindy's little sister, Mary, during a séance. I don't know if Anne Frank ever showed up, but we were able to make Mary cry. That was something.

Cindy fussed the whole time we were at the Historic Swensson Farm because she was feeling noodly. Noodly? I, on the other hand, loved the way it felt at Swensson farm. It's beautiful there, with big old trees and acres of wheat planted nearby, but I'm willing to admit it seemed possible we weren't alone.

I suppose I should mention that we snuck onto the grounds because we had no other choice. The gate was locked. Old habits are hard to break. Cindy and I have been noodling our way onto unattended properties for decades.

Since the farmhouse was locked up tight, I had to photograph the interior through a closed window, but I got a sense of what I'm missing. Showing me a house like the Swensson home without letting me inside to look around is like putting a piece of white cake with white frosting in front of me with a stout cup of coffee, and then telling me I can't eat it.

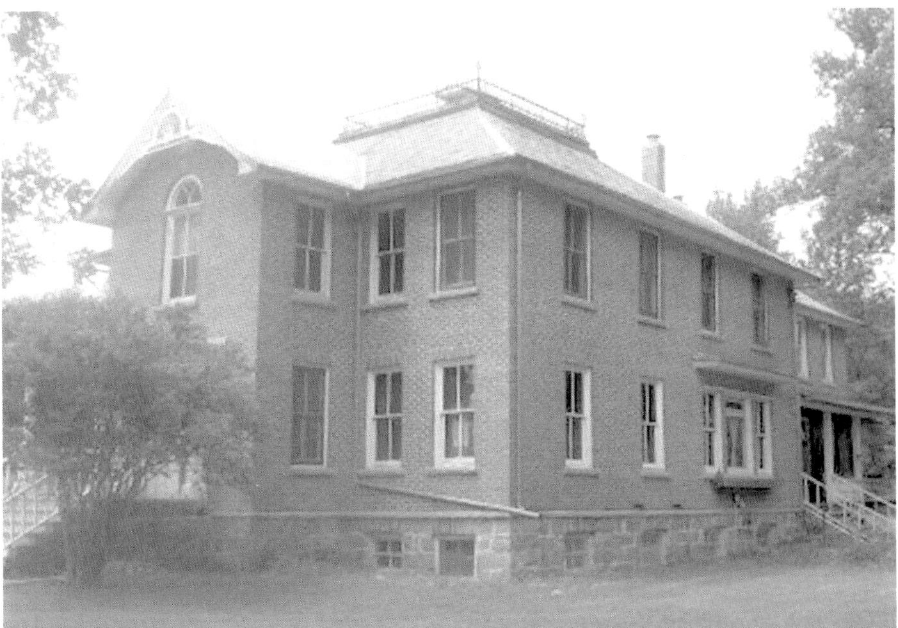

Twenty-two-room brick house at the Historic Olof Swensson Farm near Montevideo, Minnesota.

Set for the Movie *Sweetland*

Scenes from the movie *Sweetland* were filmed here at the Swensson farm. The film was winner of the Audience Award for Best Narrative Feature at the 2005 Hamptons International Film Festival. It is a warm and tender movie about the challenges facing rural Minnesota during the 1920s when anti-German sentiments were running high and farmers' incomes were running low.

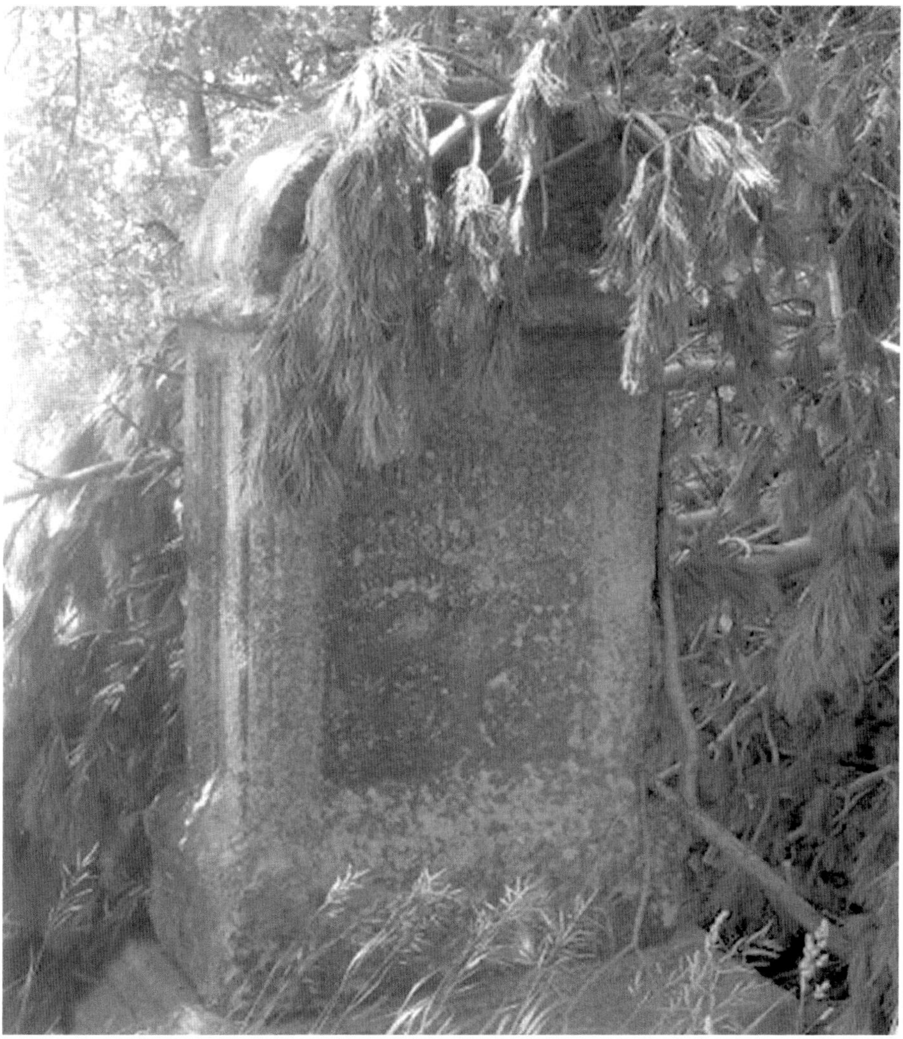

Hand-poured cement gravestone at the Historic Olof Swensson Farm near Montevideo, Minnesota.

The strong horizontal lines in the landscape of the prairie remind me of paintings by Minnesota folk artist Arnold Kramer. A retired farmer from Seaforth who retired to Wabasso, Kramer painted about four hundred paintings, which are now sprinkled across the country. The University of Minnesota dubbed him Minnesota's Grandpa Moses due to the similarity of his primitive style with that of the famous Grandma Moses from New England. The Minnesota Historical Society recently acquired one of Kramer's paintings on the merit of their strong local themes. I am especially reminded of Kramer's paintings while watching the threshing scene in *Sweetland*, with all of its antique machinery.

Cindy loved the Swensson family cemetery with its crumbling concrete headstones located across a field from the house. My little sister, Annie, says the tombstones were created from an old mold still stored in the basement of the house. Annie also said the house is filled with the original furniture and household items used by the Swensson family.

There is a legend surrounding the farm that tells of a pipe installed from the graveyard to a spot in the basement foundation, which allowed surviving family members to listen for sounds in case a newly deceased loved one was not really dead when buried. Whether it is true seems to be open for debate.

Not one to neglect the spiritual life of his family, Swensson built a chapel on the third floor of the house, enabling family and neighbors to celebrate services regularly.

The barn on the Olof Swensson farm is the largest museum-quality barn restoration in the state's history. The barn had been steadily deteriorating, and after it was bequeathed to the Chippewa County Historical Society in 1967, it was granted a new lease on life, thanks in part to public and private funding and a belief in its value in preserving the local rural history.

HISTORIC CHIPPEWA CITY IN MONTEVIDEO

Dear Diary,

I recently visited with my best friend, Cindy, who I've known since junior high. Back then, she had just moved to Wabasso from Colorado Springs and was looking for a friend. She says she thought I was fascinating (I'm adequate) because I had on these huge, cream-colored patent leather loafers with a gold chain across the top, and she had never seen anything like them before, nor had anyone else for that matter. Cindy tends to judge people by their shoes.

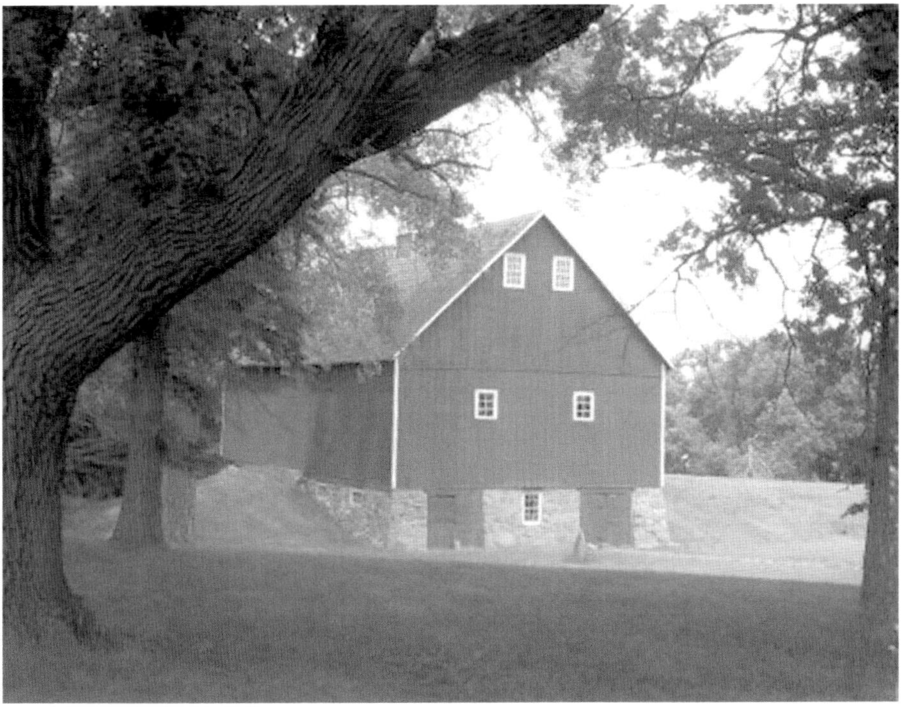

Preserved red barn on the Historic Olof Swensson Farm near Montevideo, Minnesota.

Every so often, we like to hop in the car and look at the local attractions in the western end of the Minnesota River Valley. We started out at the Millinery Shop at Pioneer Village, aka Historic Chippewa City, in Montevideo, Minnesota, where we discussed which kind of hat would have best suited us. I said I saw myself in the Roaring Twenties hanging out with Scott and Zelda Fitzgerald, and Cindy said she would have been a Gibson Girl.

Some people just refuse to grow up, and evidently Cindy is one of them—which is why we have so much fun when we're together.

At the vintage post office, I watched while Cindy committed a federal offense. I saw her take someone else's mail out of the mailbox and read it. It was very old *mail, but still…isn't that a federal offense or something?*

When she thought I wasn't paying attention, I caught her sneaking up the stairs in one of the historic houses and peeking into the attic (though this is not recommended and now we're probably in trouble). And just so you don't have to do the same thing, I'll enlighten you. There's storage up there.

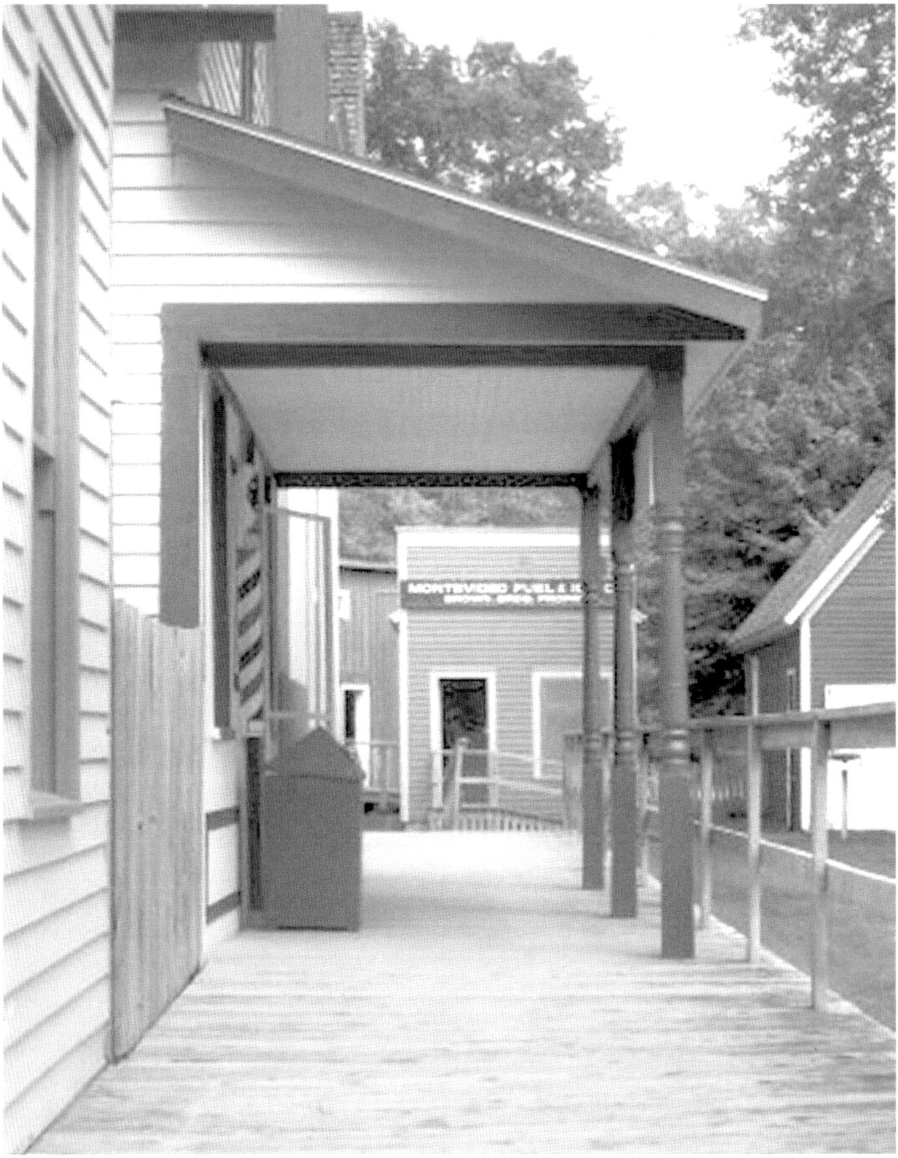

Boardwalk at the Historic Chippewa Village in Montevideo, Minnesota.

She wasn't too bad at the schoolhouse, except that she made me be the teacher. Cindy actually is a teacher. She's half a year older than me, and therefore, she thinks she's the boss of me. For the record, no one is. Well, my mom.

Just think how much fun a kid would have here! I mean, we're grown-ups and we had a fabulous time.

—Minnesota Country Mouse

The Life and Times of Judge Weiland

Pioneer of Jordan and Shakopee

Not Looking for Perfection in Jordan

Dear Diary,

I'm not looking for perfection. I much prefer quirky and interesting. And if like attracts like, that's probably why I'm so crazy about Jordan, Minnesota, located about twenty minutes south of the Twin Cities.

While Melanie was digging around in the antique shops, I was poking around where I didn't belong looking for who knows what. I wasn't disappointed in the gems I spotted. Jordan is full of little, old, imperfect buildings and old-fashioned gardens.

There were courtyards between buildings and surprising spaces along Sand Creek, which runs through the city. It couldn't have felt more like a Sunday afternoon from bygone days if it had tried. Jordan has the most wonderful small-town feeling about it.

When Melanie and I pulled into Jordan we drove past the Nicolin Mansion B&B, and she said to me, "Should we see if we can take a tour?" I objected because I didn't want to intrude, but Melanie's philosophy is to wear down her adversaries by presenting the same proposition over and over in just a little different manner each time.

We stopped in a couple of antique shops and then she lured me down the street toward the B&B. That's really all it took, because she knows I love architecture and this was no exception. The yard was inviting with large, old shade trees and a fountain.

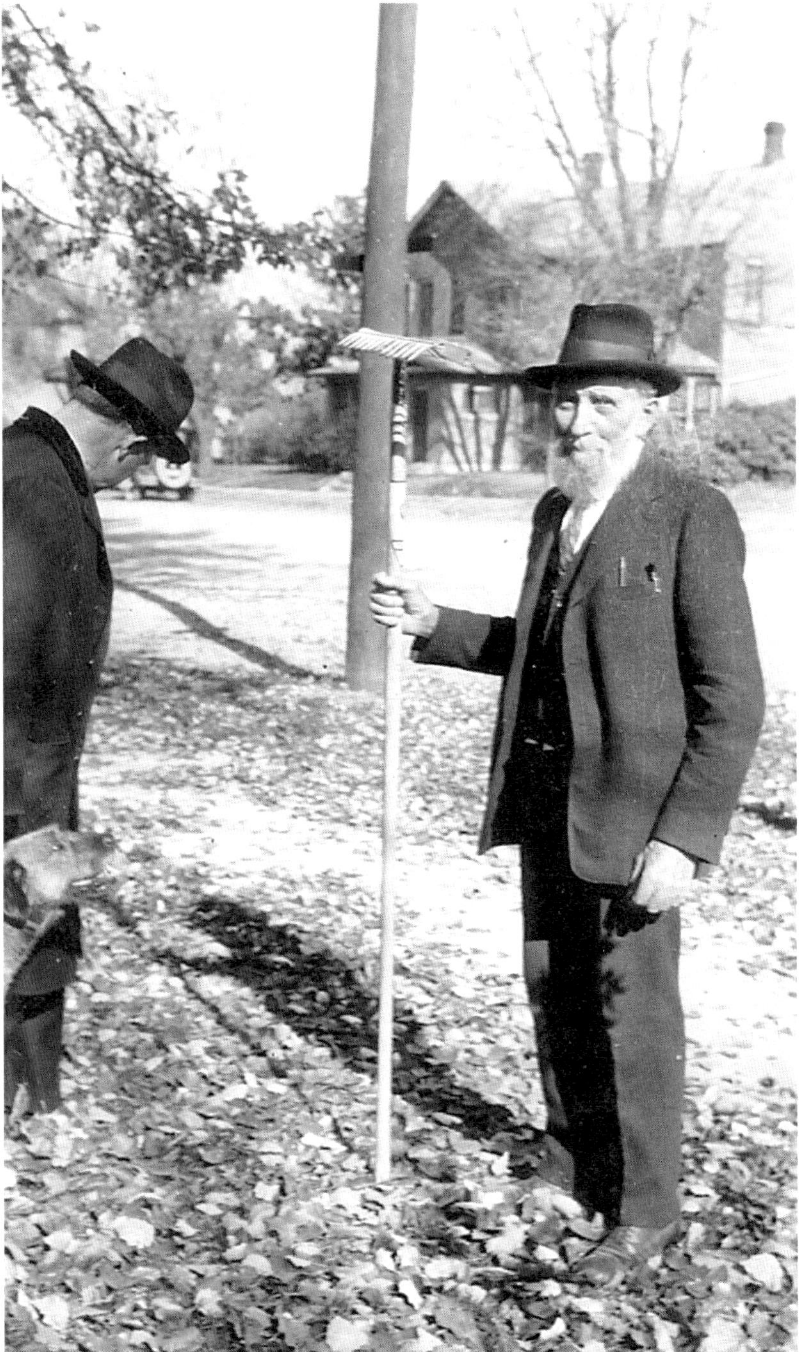

Judge Theodore Weiland, one of the men inside the bank at the time of the robbery. *Courtesy of the Gary Anderson family, Richfield, Minnesota.*

As luck would have it, the owners were working in that beautiful yard and invited us to come in. I guess what Melanie wants, Melanie gets.

What a stately home! The city of Jordan is fortunate to have such grand accommodations featuring five lavish guest rooms—all with private baths. The Nicolin Mansion B&B has a rich history and has been carefully preserved. An overnight stay here is surely a night spent in the lap of luxury.

I was looking around their most popular guest room, and I mentioned to the proprietor that I noticed there wasn't a TV and asked how people generally entertain themselves when they stay.

Even Melanie knew the answer to that. They come here for romance. *Duh. Clearly it's time for me to put Steinbeck and Faulkner back on the bookshelf and pick up a couple of Melanie's trashy dime-store novels.*

—Minnesota Country Mouse

When I told my co-worker Gary that I was writing a book about the Minnesota River Valley and that I was looking for odd and interesting stories, he took note. Gary is an avid historian with a natural curiosity about people and history. He is also lucky enough to be married to a woman with an interesting, quirky and, it seems, likeable ancestor by the name of Judge Theodore Weiland, who lived his adult life in Jordan and Shakopee at the eastern end of the Minnesota River Valley.

I don't know if it is possible to like someone who died decades before I was born, but after reading about Weiland's well-documented life in the river valley, if it is possible, then I do. I tend to have an affinity for those who start out disadvantaged and pull themselves up by their bootstraps. By the end of his busy life, Weiland had become a sharp-shootin', horse-thief-chasin', business-ownin', community-servin', family-lovin' pioneer.

He came to the Minnesota River Valley with all of his possessions strapped onto an old-fashioned telescope valise and worked on farms around the Jordan area until he had saved enough wages to start a business.

Early Life

Details of his early life are sketchy. Records show that Theodore Weiland was born in Brown County, Wisconsin, on January 15, 1849, and was raised on a farm near Fond du Lac. In 1857, he went to Green Bay and attended school for four years. Weiland's parents died when he was young, and at the age of ten, he was sent to work with a farmer who used only the most rudimentary tools for sowing and harvesting his crops. Once old enough, Weiland spent a number of years traveling between Minnesota and his home state of Wisconsin.

Weiland explored the growing community of Duluth in northeastern Minnesota while working for the Northern Pacific Railroad Company, no doubt, on his time off, grabbing a shotgun and bagging his share of the ample wildlife thriving just outside the quickly growing community.

When he finally settled in Jordan, he opened a carriage and wagon shop. This was only the beginning of a lifetime of achievements for Weiland.

On January 25, 1874, Weiland married his sweetheart, Louisa Mayer, who was born near Niagara Falls in the province of Ontario, Canada. She had moved with her family to a farm in Belle Plaine Township in southeastern Minnesota twenty years earlier. The couple soon got down to the business of raising a houseful of seven children. Louisa must have worked hard to keep up with her ambitious husband and be of service to her community. Sadly, she died of heart failure fairly young at the age of only fifty-five, having been afflicted by a number of ailments that forced her to take to her bed about a week before her death.

Ladder of Success

An obituary commemorating the honorable Judge Weiland in the March 19, 1931 edition of the *Shakopee Argus-Tribune* describes him as "a prominent, respected and highly esteemed resident and citizen." The *Jordan Independent* March 19, 1931 edition calls him "one of the remarkable men of Scott County, self-made, working his way up from comparative poverty to affluence and prominence." He began his career as a blacksmith and, by the end of his life, had served as president of the First National Bank of Shakopee.

In the course of his eighty-two years, Weiland owned an opera house and flour and feed store. His trustworthiness won him the position of marshal of Jordan in 1876. In 1904, he helped organize the People's State Bank in Jordan.

He was appointed sheriff of Scott County, a title that prompted the family to move to the river town of Shakopee, where he served for ten years. As a resident of Shakopee, Weiland served on the Board of Equalization and the Shakopee Board of Education, holding the position of president in the latter organization for a number of years. He was promoted and served as municipal judge for the last twenty years of his life.

Weiland's adult life, as it turns out, was very well documented. It is the good fortune of our generation to have history preserved in the eloquent language of bygone newspaper reporting, providing colorful and fascinating details of events. Observe the following article from the *Shakopee Argus-Tribune* of June 13, 1926, honoring Weiland:

Shakopee Bank President Once Was Called Nemesis of Horse Thieves

Few living Minnesota pioneers had a more colorful career than Theodore Weiland, 77 years old, president of the First National bank here, former mayor and former sheriff of Scott County, who began his climb to wealth and prominence as an orphan boy on a farm near Oshkosh, Wis.

As the nemesis of horse thieves while sheriff in the early days, as an adventurer of Duluth when that city was only a cluster of half dozen huts, as early exponent of modern agricultural methods, Weiland's career has been checkered and exciting.

Mr. Weiland was one of the first men in this section to promote the organization of a co-operative creamery and was instrumental in the establishment of several.

Chased Horse Thieves

In 1879, when the veteran banker became sheriff, horse thieves were active in the Northwest. They were daring, dangerous men and trailing them was a man-sized job. On one occasion Weiland miraculously escaped death in a running fight near Chaska.

"The horse thieves who operated in this community were pretty hard characters, usually from the Twin Cities," he recalled. "In those days it was easy for them to cover their trail and if they got out of the neighborhood they usually went clear. It was my duty to see that they didn't get away."

"One day I received a tip that Hank O'Keefe, a notorious character living near Shakopee, had bought a $200 horse stolen in St. Paul for $10. The St. Paul authorities were hard after him, but had failed to pick up his trail."

"My information led me to believe that O'Keefe was planning to work his way Eastward on the other side of the Minnesota River. I started out after him at night, taking with me a man who knew the horse. We overtook him in Carver County. He was driving the stolen animal with another and had a man with him."

EMPTIED HIS GUN
"When I attempted to halt them, O'Keefe jumped and ran. Drawing my revolver, I followed. It was too dark to shoot effectively and I didn't want to kill my man anyway. But he emptied his gun at me and several of his bullets missed me by only a fraction of an inch. We found him later in a physician's office being treated for gunshot wounds and he was sent to the penitentiary."

The story handed down for several generations regarding Weiland's apprehension of O'Keefe provides evidence supporting Weiland's conclusion that O'Keefe's bullets missed him by a fraction of an inch. When he returned home from the hunt, what should his wife, Louisa, see but a bullet hole in her husband's hat.

And even when Weiland wasn't in the pursuit of justice, he found himself part of an exciting story, as reported in the *Shakopee Argus-Tribune* of December 12, 1929:

LOCAL MEN DROP BANDIT TRIO
Machinegun, Shotguns, Rifles, Revolvers Harmonize in Wicked Chant as Bandits Stagger Toward Their Car. Two Dropped in Tracks in attempting to Escape. Third, Carrying Loot, Falls After Severe Shooting.
Receive Boisterous Reception on Visit to Local First National Bank
Armed Citizens Get into Action and Stage Gun Battle on Street
Three bank bandits, William (Bud) McNearney, George Larkin and Paul Morris strolled nonchalantly into the First National Bank here at 9:50 on Monday morning, ordered the occupants, Theo Weiland, Sr., John Theim, Lucile Schwartz, and E.J. Huber to lie face downward on the floor and then proceeded to ransack the place.

Found Vault Closed
Finding the vault closed one of the men ordered Ed Huber to his feet to manipulate and open the huge vault door. This done, they entered and appropriated the two bundles of $1 bills, totaling $1700, which had been laid out for their convenience. One of the trio carried a large white sack in which to place the loot. This bag, however, was left on the bank floor when, a moment later, the shooting started.

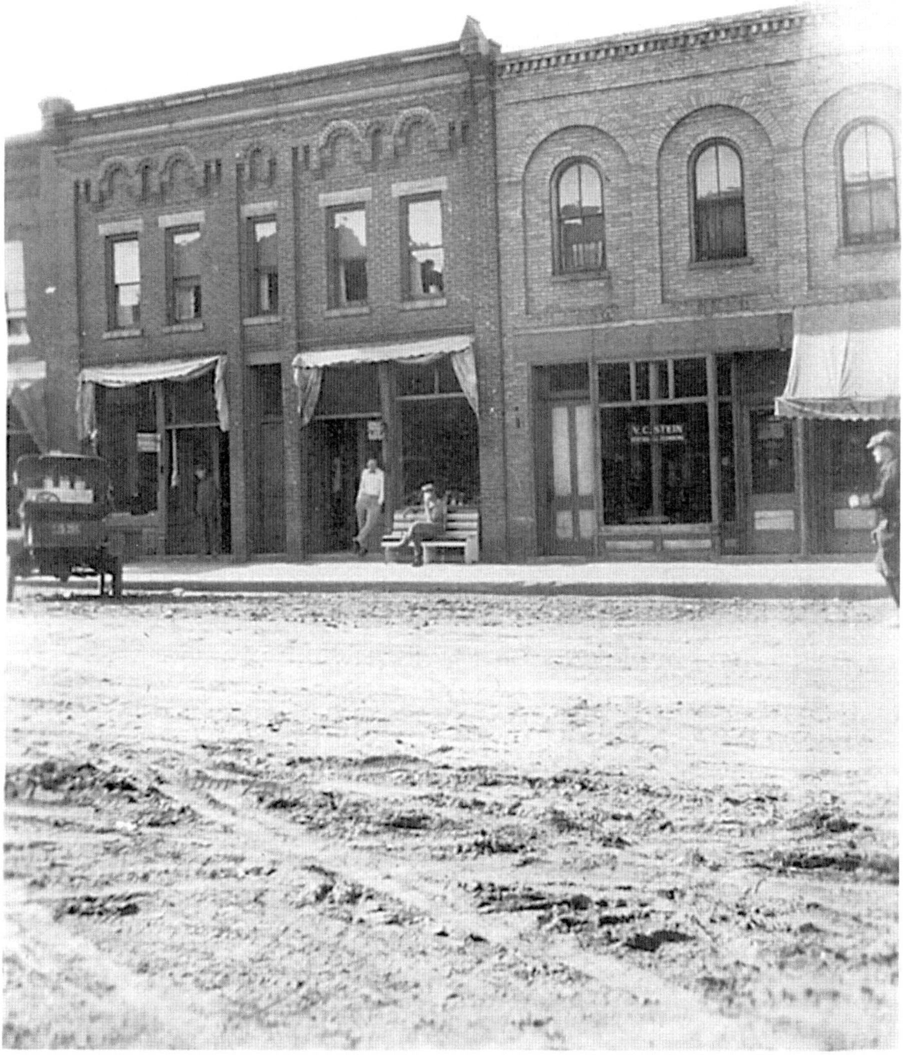

Shakopee Bank robbed in December 1929. *Courtesy of the Gary Anderson family, Richfield, Minnesota.*

R.L. Brown Gets Man

When the planted money was picked up within and no other currency was in sight the trio started to leave the bank. The first man out was met by the bank of a shot gun in the hands of Deputy Lester Brown, head of the Minnesota Bankers' Protective Association, and Sheriff Jos. Wickman who arranged the trap. The man on his way to their car parked in front of the bank, dropped as he crossed the sidewalk and rolled over into the street with his head and shoulders remaining on the curb.

Knew They Were Trapped

Within the bank Theo. Weiland, who with Henry Marschall, a patron, was in the business chamber at the rear of the building, said one of the two remaining men realized their predicament and shouted, "We're trapped, let 'em have it."

Leave Bank Through Rear Door

One of the men, McNearney, carried the bundles of currency in his arm leaving the white sack on the floor. The two, seeking to avoid gun fire, darted out the rear of the bank. Information was shouted to Lester Brown who, with Frank Deutsch, ran around to the rear of the bank. The bandit accompanying McNearney had drawn two revolvers. As the pair raced up the alley toward highway No. 5, Brown grazed McNearney but did not drop him. Reaching the gangway between the Shakopee Drug Co. and Teidt's restaurant, the pair made a dash to return to First St. where a posse of armed local men had assembled in waiting for their prey.

Return to Car

Coming out between the two buildings onto the sidewalk, the men made a wild dash for their car where the first of the trio was lying in his blood.

One Dropped in Tracks

It was McNearney carrying the money who succeeded in reaching the car. The second man was dropped in front of Strunk's Drug Store as Sheriff Wickman standing in the center of First St. and directly opposite the bank opened a volley of shot on him.

As McNearney scrambled into the car Chas. D. Brown armed with a shoulder machinegun left his station near the car opposite the bank and took a position at the intersection of First and Lewis Sts., where he let go at the rear glass and ripping into the upholstery.

Gregor Hartmann, who had perched himself in the second story of the Hartmann Market directly opposite the bank, drew a bead on McNearney and a bullet from his high-calibre deer rifle through the jaw of his victim. McNearney, driven from the car under heavy rifle fire, again entered the bank still carrying the loot.

Leaves Trail of Blood

A trail of blood followed in his wake as he rushed through the bank and up the alley for the highway and probable safety. This time another gun was brought into play. It was Al Tiedt, who, when he saw McNearney re-enter the bank, grabbed his twelve gauge shot gun and took a position at the rear porch of his restaurant.

Tiedt Gets McNearney

His man came up the alley, still carrying the loot, after having hidden a moment in the basement entry to Strunk's Drug store. As he reached the garage at the rear of V.C. Stein's plumbing establishment, Al shouted and the bandit retraced his steps and appeared at the opposite end of the garage. Then he fired and McNearney fell against a dog house at the south end of the garage. Here he dropped the loot and took to his feet, moving from the gun fire in rapid pace. As he crossed the alley running south Tiedt fired again, the man staggered a little but continued toward a chicken coop on the north side of the alley where, after a third shot from Tiedt's gun he fell against the window of the frame structure and there he remained.

Shells in Car

In the large sedan in which the bandits arrived on the scene, were found a clothes line, extra license plates, a grip containing a large quantity of ammunition, and a quantity of moonshine. The victims were removed to the Shakopee hospital, where their wounds were dressed. Later Larkin and Morris were removed to Mudeura Sanitarium where they were placed under guard. McNearney most critically injured was also under guard at the local hospital.

Two Identified

Two of the bandits, Larkin and McNearney, were identified by Chief E.J. Murnane as St. Paul police characters. McNearney was arrested on several occasions and has served time in St. Cloud reformatory to which institution he was sent Mary 23, 1925. He is 30 years old, married and has one daughter. His father, mother, wife and daughter were with him Monday night in the hospital here.

Larkin has also served time in the St. Cloud reformatory. He is 32 years old and is a taxicab driver. Morris was not identified. He gave his home as Chicago.

Chas. Manaige Active

Having sensed the approaching conflict, Chas. Manaige, aged Civil War veteran, driving down First St. with his white horse and rattling buggy whipped his steed into action and raced up Lewis St. shouting at the top of his familiar voice. "The bank is being robbed, get your guns." Just as Paul Revere did, and exactly as the venerable veteran conducted himself in the historic Civil War, he remained within the danger zone, unmindful of his own danger, attracting a multitude of armed citizens.

Heavy Shooting

Rifles banked, pistols cracked and a machine gun spat in wicked harmony. Men hurried from all directions to the scene. Henry Verkennes, Geo. Beguhl, Frank Deutch, Bernard Jansen, Roy Miller, Jos. Klinkhammer, F.J. Gross, J.H. Ring, police chief, and a host of men who were not readily discerned, flashed weapons and waited in readiness for an opportunity to open fire. There is but slight evidence of an exchange of shots and that was in the direction of the Hartmann building, a bullet having shattered the plate glass window. One of the bank windows was also pierced and the bullet lodged in the ceiling.

Cars parked along the street settled down on flat tires, wind shields took on odd designs and car bodies suddenly developed gaping pores.

Chas. Brown Gets "Tip"

The trap which resulted in gruesome and sanguinary conflict was arranged under the direction of Chas. D. Brown and Sheriff Jos. Weckman. Several days ago Brown picked up a "tip" that a bank robbery was scheduled to occur Tuesday in Scott County. Where the robbery would be staged was not known. Acting on this "tip" Brown posted all the banks in this county.

At 2 o'clock Monday morning, Brown received another tip from underworld operatives. This one was detailed and accurate. It was to be the First National Bank at Shakopee, Brown said. He then informed bank officials and other operatives and as a result all were in readiness for the affair that followed. About five minutes before the bandits arrived Brown and an assistant, George Suserns, were in their positions opposite the bank.

Bandits Arrive

Soon after the trap was set and Sheriff Weckman and his men were posted, two men walked leisurely down the street toward the bank. At the same time a large sedan went down the street, passed the bank, continued a block beyond, then turned around, came back and parked in front of the bank just as the two men entered. C.C. Brown knew these were the bandits and every armed man on the street got his signal of recognition. It was only necessary then to wait and to steel their nerves for gunfire.

Bank Officials Very Grateful
Credit Given Deputies and Citizens for Bravery in Monday's Battle

Officials of the First National Bank here are loud in their praise of the citizens of Shakopee and the Sheriff and his Deputies who faced the bandit trio who attempted to rob that bank Monday morning. "Much of the credit for the capture of the band goes to the men of this city, the Sheriff and his Deputies" one of the officials said.

Lester Brown was particularly mentioned, and every man was given credit and a share of the honors. Bank officials have expressed their thankfulness and appreciation and have requested this paper to reiterate their feelings of honor and respect for every man who aided the capture.

They are mindful of the important part played by Chas. D. Brown and his associate Geo. Susens, but they are confident that without the aid of Scott County officials and the Shakopee citizenry, the outcome would not have been as effective.

Those who assisted in establishing the identity of the bandit trio were also mentioned and it is their hope that no one concerned in the affair has gone unremembered or unknown.

Because of the great number of men active during the holdup it would be impossible to enumerate them all, but each is held in high esteem by the employees and officials of the bank.

Weiland died on March 18, 1931. The newspapers recorded his death in detail, regretfully informing the public that their local hero suffered from a severe case of eczema weeks earlier, causing him a great deal of discomfort, and that he was finally defeated by pneumonia.

What was the secret to Weiland's success? Was it brains, disposition, timing? Or could it have been ambition, trustworthiness and his work ethic? Or was it the support and encouragement of a good woman? Whatever the case, Weiland made a place for himself in Minnesota River Valley history as a pioneer and played a major role in shaping the charming communities of Jordan and Shakopee.

Turner Hall, Murals, World War I and Prisoners of War

By Terry Sveine

Hermann

Dear Diary,

While Melanie and I were interviewing Terry Sveine of the New Ulm CVB, we got to hear the history of why Hermann, a Cheruscan chieftain who lived in ancient times, has a huge monument in New Ulm, Minnesota. Alas, the interview was lost due to operator error.

On special occasions, when I was a little, my parents would load up the old green station wagon with us kids and haul us to New Ulm, singing all the way. "I've Been Working on the Railroad" and "It Ain't Gonna Rain No More, No More"…

Anyway, we always stopped at the Hermann Monument, "Hermann's Heights" my dad called it, and we'd wear ourselves out climbing to the top of this incredibly huge structure. I suppose my folks wanted us good and worn-out for the long trip home.

I feel bad that I didn't get a photo of the monument, but New Ulm has so many places to visit, Melanie and I ended up burning daylight faster than we intended. We have no option but to come back. And maybe this time I can get an interview with Terry that my computer won't destroy. This guy knows a lot of stuff!

—Minnesota Country Mouse

You may wonder how the varied entities in this essay's title can possibly be related, but if you bear with me, the very real connections will reveal themselves.

German Immigrants

New Ulm was founded by two groups of German immigrants, both of whom wanted to create "a Utopian German community on the American wilderness." The first group of settlers were Germans living in Chicago who sent an advance party to New Ulm in 1854 who then stayed the winter to hold their claim. The next year, about two hundred of the Chicago-based group joined them. In 1856, a group of Germans living in Cincinnati heard of the first group and asked to join them. They were welcome, as starting a new community was difficult and expensive, and soon five-hundred-plus new people joined the original settlers.

The Cincinnati Group

The Cincinnati group was "the Turners" which, as their name indicated, included "turning," or gymnastics, as part of their "A Sound Mind, In a Sound Body" philosophy. Elements of socialism and liberalism were part of the "practical Turnerism," and they prided themselves on being freethinkers who could make choices based on their own free will and not be led where they didn't want to go. There has been a Turner Hall in New Ulm on the same location since 1857.

The current building consists of two parts—one from 1954 and the other from 1873—and it is evident which one is older by the more elaborate architectural style. In the basement of the older building are paintings of scenes from Germany done by an itinerant Italian painter in 1879. They are very nice but were not always visible for us to enjoy as we do today!

World War I

In 1917, when America was about to enter World War I, the Turners were by and large against American involvement. In July, after a parade through town, a large rally was held on the grounds of Turner Hall's park in central New Ulm. With great paraphrasing and simplifying here, what was generally said, aside from general exhortations against the war, was that if someone was drafted he should try and get in a branch of the military where he wouldn't have to go to the German front and shoot his cousin. Both federal and state spies were in this audience and at other area speeches that were given. The result was that by August, our mayor, city attorney and county auditor had been removed from office by the governor's Committee of Public Safety as being traitorous. A large banner hung over our neighboring Sleepy Eye's Main Street (fifteen miles west) that said "Berlin: 15 Miles East" expressed some of the concern of New Ulm's perceived attitude toward Germany during the war.

Soon after 1917, the murals were painted over. While it appears to be unknowable exactly when and how this happened, the biggest consensus is that it was done to prove loyalty to the United States and to placate some of the criticism the entire town was getting over being "too German." Other factors regarding the over-painting had to do with changing decorative tastes and concerns about growing damage to the murals from being painted on plaster that was applied directly to the limestone outer walls and was now starting to disintegrate.

Prisoners of War

By 1944, near the end of World War II, New Ulm had gone from being a town suspected of, and even led by, German sympathizers during World War I to obviously being considered quite loyal, since it was chosen to house a prisoner of war camp for German soldiers! The land in Flandrau Park across the Cottonwood River from the main park was the former home of a transients' camp in the Depression of the early 1930s and later as a housing area for workers on CCC projects in the later 1930s. It was deemed adequate to house about 140 German Air Corpsmen who were kept there until the end of the war. These prisoners were forced to work at area farms, industries and food-packing plants during the war. There were no serious episodes of escape, and there were general good relations between them and the locals.

Back to Turner Hall

Loyalties had been proven and emotions had settled down, but still the murals sat painted over and unknown to most of the new generations who regularly used Turner Hall.

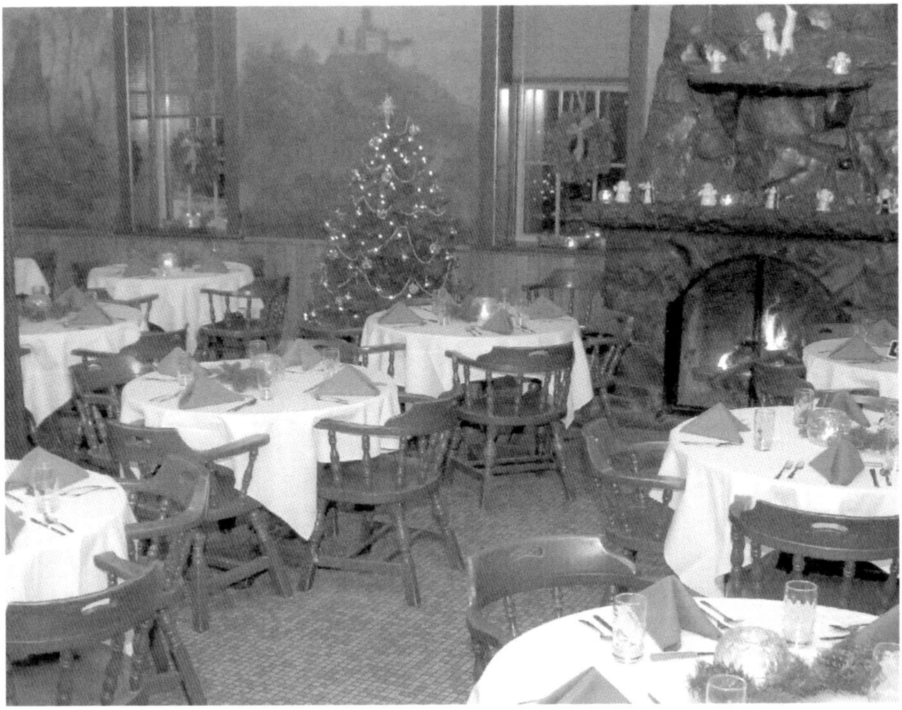

Turner Hall in New Ulm, Minnesota, was built in 1865 after the original building was destroyed in the U.S.-Dakota Conflict of 1862. *Courtesy of the New Ulm Historical Society.*

Finally, in 1998, Turner Hall was interested in recapturing these lost treasures, and with grant money, donations and membership commitments, efforts were made to restore the historic murals. Turner manager Rick Runck worked with Mr. Carroll Elijiah (with some help, but mainly on his own), and Carroll spent about two years with solvent, cotton swabs and 250,000 feet of sticky duct tape (!) removing the old and revealing gorgeous murals. The cost of this restoration has been estimated at between $150,000 and $170,000.

Once again, the murals are visible to visitors and Turner members alike, and they connect a long history of immigration, pride, loyalty and unfair charges of treachery. Enjoy this interesting vestige of New Ulm's past and appreciate the work and emotions that it represents.

Courtesy of Terry Sveine
Chamber of Commerce
New Ulm, Minnesota
2009

Millions of Cats

Time Travel

Dear Diary,

I'd be hard pressed to tell you what my favorite experience was while visiting New Ulm in the Minnesota River Valley, but I know visiting Sven and Ole's Books was near the top.

Hailing from Minnesota, my friend Melanie and I were fairly certain we were going to enjoy whatever Sven and Ole's had to offer. For me, it was the discovery of two Anne Tyler books to add to my collection, and for Melanie, it was a copy of Wanda Gag's book, Millions of Cats, *a classic for kids.*

Now, are you ready for the really good part of this story? Wanda Gag grew up just a few blocks away in a truly lovely house that you can tour. The Gags' charming house looks like the kind of place that would foster creativity. We had to visit it!

According to her biography, Wanda's life was not as fortunate as the architecture would imply. There were bumps in the road.

Visiting hours are fairly limited, and we missed them, so we walked around the outside and admired how impeccably the Wanda Gag house has been preserved.

Now this *is the way I like to experience history. It was like a little bit of time travel.*

—Minnesota Country Mouse

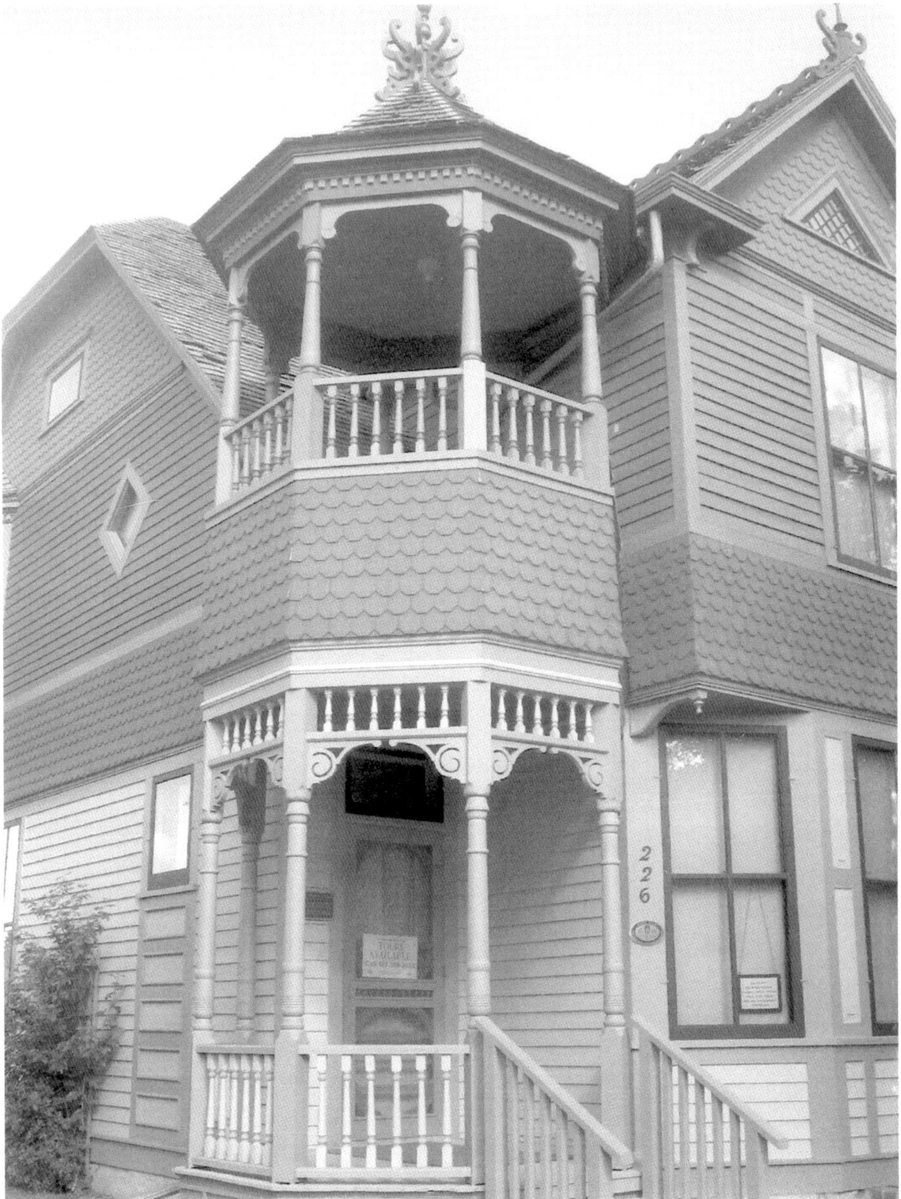

Wanda Gag House, located in New Ulm, Minnesota.

The first person to ever read Wanda Gag's book, *Millions of Cats*, to me was Captain Kangaroo. Back before kindergarten began occupying our days, my twin brother and I sat on the old braided rug in front of our black-and-white television set and gave the Captain our complete attention. There on the TV screen, big as life, was Captain Kangaroo launching into a story as only a TV icon could. We were rapt as the Captain chanted, "Hundreds of cats, thousands of cats, and millions and billions and trillions of cats."

I'm not sure if we ever had *Millions of Cats* in our book collection dominated by Dr. Seuss, but our little brick library in the tiny community of nearby Wabasso housed it. As a small girl growing up relatively isolated on the family farm, I couldn't have imagined that author and illustrator Wanda Gag had grown up a mere fifty miles from me in New Ulm along the Minnesota River.

I have always judged a book by its cover, but my propensity to form a storyline based on appearances doesn't seem to end there. The first time I saw the delightful Queen Anne home Wanda Gag grew up in on the corner of North Washington Street in New Ulm, I was certain she was one of the luckiest girls in Minnesota. Imagine it. Her father, Anton (Gaag) Gag, was a Bohemian woodcarver, painter and photographer who built this gem of a house, and her mother was a gifted storyteller, sharing old world fairy tales and family history. It all seemed so romantic.

Black-and-white photos of Wanda show a pixie of a girl. One of my favorites was taken about 1916, when Wanda was an art student at the Minneapolis School of Art. She is posing in an artist's beret and smock, holding a huge painter's palette and paintbrush. A curtain of crimped bangs hanging just over her left eye, she is looking, unsmiling, into the camera. Why didn't *I* think of having my picture taken like that? In my head I had made up the narrative that things came very easily to her. And then I learned the real story.

Little Wanda

Wanda Hazel Gag was born in New Ulm on March 11, 1893. She and her parents lived in an apartment between a saloon and a blacksmith shop infested with bedbugs. Her poor little arms and legs were covered with bites, and when the Gags moved to a larger home, the bedbugs moved with them.

Wanda's mother, Elizabeth (Lissi) Biebl Gag, and her father, Anton, set up a photograph studio in their home. They met in 1888 when, as a teenager, Lissi applied for a job as assistant to Anton. Anton must have been taken by

Lissi's sweet disposition and bird-like countenance. Lissi, on the other hand, was attracted to the job by the "Help Wanted" sign displayed in the studio window, seeking an individual who was "artistic." Her only other work experience had been as a maid in the local hotel.

The busiest day at the studio was Sunday, when families gussied up in their best clothes for church. Wanda's mother proved to be a tremendous asset to Anton, exhibiting a gift for making children sit still and smile. She was clever, pretty and amiable. The couple worked together for four years and tied the knot in 1892.

Anton and Lissi were compassionate people with an affinity for the poor. Anton's escape from the tyranny inflicted by the police and other power-mongers in nineteenth-century Bohemia made him tenderhearted toward the less fortunate. As she grew older, Wanda tried to imagine the internal conflict her father must have felt as he worked on commission, painting a large mural representing the attack of New Ulm by the Native Americans. She knew he felt compassion for the settlers who were attacked, but he also loved the Indians and felt they had been wronged.

As a result of his reputation for generosity, individuals who employed his skills as a painter-decorator were able to take advantage of him, paying house painter wages for a craftsman's work. As she grew into adulthood, Wanda felt that her father's good nature led large, impersonal organizations, most notably the local churches he was hired to decorate and paint murals in, to take advantage of him.

Wanda's mother, Lissi, is remembered for providing breakfast to wandering gypsies, a gesture viewed with some contempt by other citizens of the community. Nevertheless, the Gags were freethinkers and followed their hearts.

IMPRACTICAL ARTIST

In 1894, Anton built a house worthy of an artist for his quickly growing household. The Queen Anne–style architecture, with its delightful turret and fish scale shingle siding, was a work of art. Unfortunately, the Gags had to sell the house without ever occupying it in order to pay their debts. After working and saving their money for several years, they were able to finally buy back their beautiful home and move in just before Wanda turned four.

The neighbors may have secretly admired the beauty of the house's embellishments, but they vocalized their disdain for its impractical design. The house had a well-lit studio with large windows and skylights. Everyone knew skylights leaked, and this house was no different. Pans and buckets were kept handy to catch the drips during rainstorms. But Anton was an artist, and he needed an artist's studio for his craft.

Four-year-old Wanda loved the new house and was her father's most loyal fan, following him around as he did his photography and painting. She watched quietly as he painted still lifes, confident that she would be rewarded with fruit from the bowl sitting as a prop on a nearby table, and now appearing in her father's painting. Her father allowed Wanda to study the art books lining the shelf of a built-in bookcase but warned her not to copy the work. Her paintings and drawings should reflect her own fresh view of the world.

Anton was pleased by Wanda's imagination. "Na, my little Wanda is dreaming again!"

Inspired by Tales

Wanda was soon joined by four sisters and one brother—Howard Anthony Jerome, Asta Theopolis, Thusnelda Blondine (Tussy), Stella Lona and Dehli Maryland. The children were raised in a liberal household with the freedom to express themselves. The provincial nature of the community, with its strict German background and small-town talk, made it difficult for such an unusual and artistic family to fit in.

The Gags spoke only German in their home, and Wanda did not learn to speak English until she entered grade school. In the fourth grade, she was allowed to check books out of the school library. Two books helped her make important life decisions not many years later. The first, *Hans Brinker: The Silver Skates* by Mary Mapes Dodge, written in 1865, tells of a brother and sister who help support their family as their father recovers from an accident. The family is looked down upon by the community because of their poor economic status.

The second, the *Five Little Peppers* series, written by Margaret Sidney in the late 1800s, tells of a family who learns to stay together and keep the wolf from the door after their father's death. The Pepper family also endures financial hardship and is eventually rescued by a wealthy benefactor. During the hard times, the oldest daughter, Polly, remains bright and cheerful, with a special attachment to her baby sister, Phronsie.

In an example of life imitating art, Wanda's father began suffering from aching legs after all the hours he spent standing while he painted. Meanwhile, her mother was growing plump, and it became obvious that another baby was on the way. Baby Flavia Betty Salome was born on May 24, 1907, while Anton was away working on a commission to paint a church in Mankato. Without a vehicle to travel the thirty miles back and forth to his work, Anton was gone for long stretches of time, arriving home only rarely during his out-of-town employment.

Wanda's father began growing very tired and coughing a lot. He eventually became too tired to work and was diagnosed with tuberculosis, a result, the doctors concluded, from working in cold, damp cathedrals.

Wanda's mother recovered poorly after the baby was born and was too weak to care for her. Wanda took over the care of baby Flavia, nicknamed Flopsy, and became devoted to her.

Anton passed away on May 22, 1908, when Wanda was only fourteen years old. He had always encouraged Wanda in her desire to become an artist in her own right and, even on his deathbed, invoked her to continue carrying out the work he had started. He said, "*Was der Papa nicht thun kont, muss die Wanda halt fertig machen*," meaning, "What Papa has left undone, Wanda will have to do."

KEEPING THE FAMILY TOGETHER

There was a very small sum of insurance money with which to support the family after Anton's death, and the family collected eight dollars a month from welfare. The Gags struggled to pay their bills. Wanda's mother, Lissi, remained ill and unable to work outside the home. The care of the household and responsibility of earning an income fell to Wanda.

Wanda was pressured by neighbors to leave school and get a job, but she had other ideas. They offered to adopt the children, but Wanda's prevailing loyalty to her family, like her hero Polly in *The Five Little Peppers*, kept the family together.

She began selling her artwork locally and marketing her writing and drawings for greeting cards and calendars. Many of Wanda's illustrations were purchased and published by the Minneapolis Journal's *Journal Junior*, a Sunday supplement for youngsters.

She managed to graduate from high school and taught for several years in nearby Springfield. Once the next two sisters in line had graduated from high school and accepted positions as teachers, Wanda felt she could move to the Twin Cities to further her own education. She won an art scholarship enabling her to attend the St. Paul School of Art from 1913 to 1914. In 1914, she enrolled at the Minneapolis School of Art, attending until 1917. Wanda's mother, Lissi, died in 1916, and Wanda moved her school-age siblings in with her.

Rumors

During her first academic year in St. Paul, rumors made their way to Wanda from New Ulm speculating that Wanda's studies were being bankrolled by unscrupulous men; these rumors left her deeply hurt. It was true that she had begun enjoying the company of men but insisted they view her as important as they viewed themselves.

In the summer of 1917, she got her first job illustrating the children's book *A Child's Book of Folk-Lore* and earned a scholarship to the Art Students League in New York, studying there for a year. Wanda's experience with being poor influenced the journals she chose for her work, favoring socialist magazines like *The Liberator* and *New Masses*.

After graduation from art school, Wanda enjoyed a successful career as a fashion illustrator and dreamed of traveling to Germany but chose instead to send money back home to the Gag children. Wanda began writing manuscripts for possible children's books and sent the longhand copies to her sister in Minneapolis to type. She neglected, however, to send illustrations with the stories submitted to publishers, and the manuscripts ended up in the rejection box.

In 1923, Wanda decided to paint only what she wanted and left her job in New York to spend summers at a country home in Connecticut and, later, in the New Jersey countryside. Her significant other, Earle Marshall Humphreys, spent summers with her there. In order to prevent talk of impropriety, she purchased an inexpensive wedding band to wear.

Wanda worked hard and was eventually rewarded with her own art show at the Wehye Gallery in New York City in 1926. She won the admiration of the art world. Another turning point in Wanda's career came in 1928, when her well-known book *Millions of Cats* was published. She continued to publish children's books, drawings and lithographs until her death in 1946.

The Terrible Story of Little Annie Mary

Southwestern Minnesota's Most Famous Ghost

Once, back when I was very small, our family took a rare trip to Alexandria in central Minnesota to spend a weekend with my mom's college roommate at her lake home. Such luxury! We kids put on our swimsuits and raced to the beach under the wide-open sky.

I had recently mastered the art of holding my breath and swimming under water, and I was practicing this new skill in earnest. Take a big breath, hold it, stick my head underwater and wiggle like a fish, then pop up for more air. The breath-holding and wiggling like a fish were going okay, but there was one fateful pop-up that still haunts me.

After getting fairly confident with the whole routine, I popped up only to find myself in a wooden box with no way out. There were wooden boards inches above my head and on either side of me. I was completely disoriented. I let out a horrible shriek, which bounced off the walls of my tomb. I kept on screaming in terror until I heard my dad ask, "Where is she?" which was precisely what *I* wanted to know.

I hadn't realized my loved ones were so nearby, because I had the sense that I had left the world as I knew it.

"She's under the dock."

I was? In a moment my mom's beautiful face appeared before me. "Hold your breath," she told me and then ducked me under the water and back into broad daylight, where everyone had stopped swimming to look at me.

I only mention this story because I think I felt, if only for a moment, what poor little Annie Mary Twente from Brown County may have experienced.

The legend of Annie Mary's short life and strange death is told and retold in southwestern Minnesota, and I admit, it has captured my attention. My former Wabasso High School locker-mate, Audrey, whose family knows how much she hates the story of poor Annie Mary, each year receives a Halloween and Valentine's Day card with the initials A.M. printed as a return address. Someone has a dark side.

Annie Mary Twente was born October 14, 1880. She died of diphtheria, also known as "lung fever," at the age of six on October 26, 1886, on a farm near Hanska, Minnesota.

THE STRANGLING ANGEL OF CHILDREN

Between 1876 and 1905, diphtheria occurred in epidemic proportions in the state, usually affecting children. Within this time frame, almost one-third of the deaths recorded in Minnesota were those of children under the age of five. Parents sometimes delayed naming their children for several years, perhaps due to superstition, knowing that they could lose one, or their entire family, with one bout of the infection.

Diphtheria is the Greek word meaning "leather" or "pair of leather scrolls" and was years ago referred to as "the Strangling Angel of Children." The disease was named thus due to the development of a pseudo-membrane that covered the mucous lining in the respiratory system, extending into the lungs. The membrane would become thick and gray, causing problems with breathing and swallowing. If a physician tried to remove the membrane, it would cause excessive bleeding. Another obvious symptom of the illness was excessive swelling of the neck, referred to as "bull neck." But the illness wasn't limited to the respiratory system. Toxins traveled around the body, causing heart inflammation and paralysis of the throat, lungs, eyes and breathing muscles.

Once struck with diphtheria, victims who didn't survive the disease typically died in less than a week. If a child was lucky enough to survive the initial illness, he or she was still susceptible to death weeks later from heart attack or paralysis. It may be the paralysis associated with diphtheria that created the confusion surrounding Annie Mary's death.

In March 1873, the State of Minnesota passed a law requiring communities to have a board of health. Every three months, a round of inspections of local residences was conducted, and a report was filed with the State Board of Health. In 1880, the State Board of Health published a report identifying the cause of diphtheria as filth. The board suggested disinfecting a home through sunlight, pure air and artificial disinfectants, which could prove as lethal as the disease itself if inhaled.

In 1890, Emil von Behring, a Prussian scientist, discovered an anti-toxin to prevent diphtheria. Von Behring found that certain animal blood contained an anti-toxin that, when processed correctly, could be injected into humans. For his success, he was awarded the first Nobel Prize in Physiology or Medicine in 1901. By 1912, a vaccine had been developed to prevent the disease. The vaccine was made available to the public in 1920 and began to be administered to children in the United States, reducing diphtheria to the present-day level of outbreaks consisting of only about five cases annually.

But this was far too late for Annie Mary.

Colorful Father

Annie Mary's father, Richard Twente, brought his family to Brown County, Minnesota, from Kentucky in the 1880s. He brought with him a religion foreign to the local residents and a brilliant, if not somewhat disturbed, mind. Less is known about his wife, Elizabeth (Lizzie).

Twente purchased 160 acres for $1,140 in August 1884, where he farmed and sold nursery stock. In 1918, he published and copyrighted an educational pamphlet about planting fruit trees. A physically powerful man, he designed and built a three-level barn and granary that is currently listed on the National Register of Historic Places.

Twente, his wife and four daughters erected the buildings with little outside help. The granary included a scale and hoist and belt system for handling the grain. The upper level had seven bins for storage. In addition, he and his family built a two-level hog barn.

The legend of Annie Mary's family includes speculation that Twente suffered from mental illness, throwing fits of rage that frightened his family. He was admitted to Minnesota's first state hospital on several occasions. The hospital, located in St. Peter in the Minnesota River Valley, opened for the treatment of mental illness in 1866 following state legislative approval. Its purpose was to empty jails of those suffering from mental illness. Soon, however, the hospital was so full that additional facilities were built in Rochester and Fergus Falls.

A lingering tale tells how Twente bullied his family into a sleigh on a subzero day and raced across an open field, horses frothing, while the family begged to be taken home. Twente had no destination in mind, they say, and eventually relented after fear of freezing brought him to his senses.

It is unlikely his state of mind improved with the death of a child.

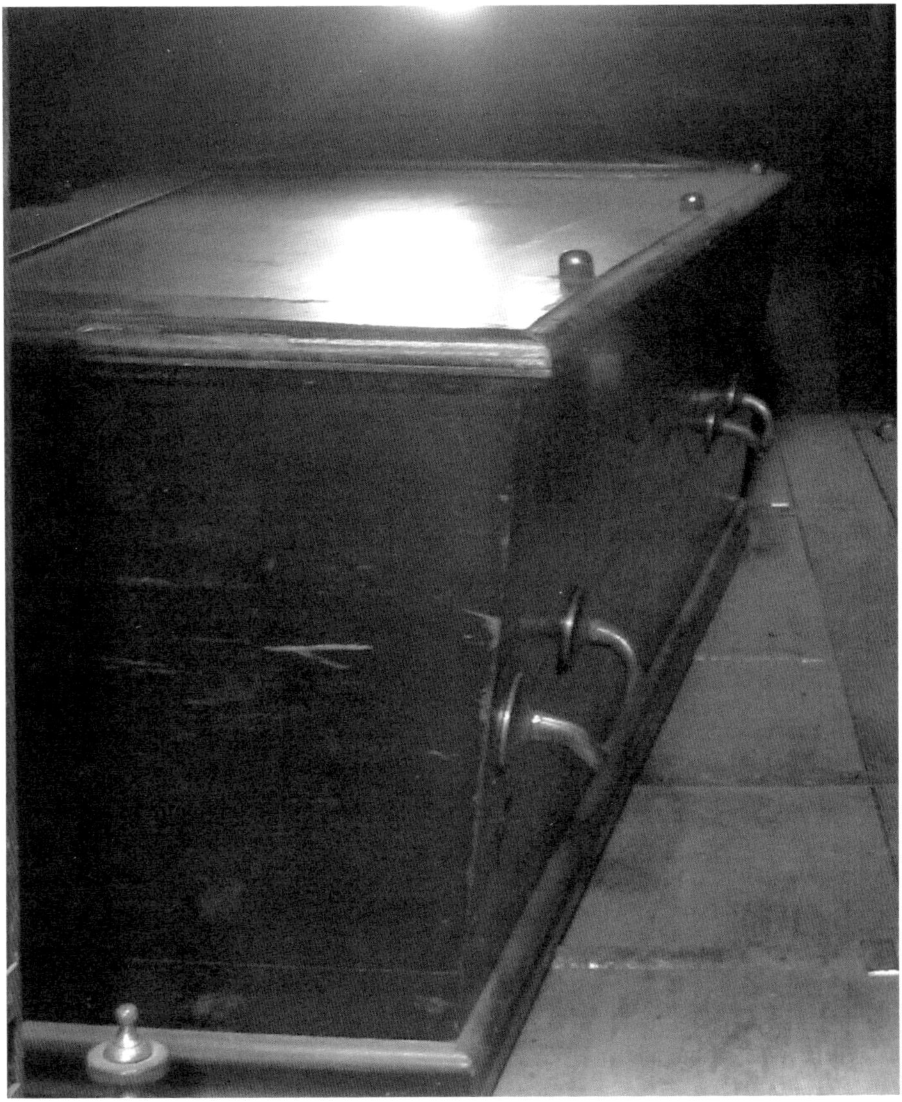

Antique casket.

ANNIE MARY DIES

Six-year-old Annie Mary, according to her death certificate filed with Brown County, succumbed to diphtheria two weeks after her birthday. She most likely struggled to breathe and eventually suffered paralysis from the toxins left in her body by her illness. This paralysis would have made it very difficult to determine whether she was deceased. The stories handed down through several generations of relatives and neighbors suggest that Annie Mary's mother, Elizabeth, was not convinced the child was dead before she was buried.

Given his carpentry skills, it is most likely that Twente built Annie Mary's casket with his own hands. Annie Mary was laid to rest in the Iberia cemetery in Stark Township to the north of the family's farm. This didn't seem to satisfy Twente, as he exhumed little Annie Mary and brought her home to bury at the highest point on his farm.

Grief makes people do strange things. Perhaps it was due to Twente's unstable mind, or maybe Elizabeth needed one last glimpse of her little daughter, but whatever the reason, the cover was lifted off the casket and the Twentes saw a garish sight.

According to legend, the inside of the casket showed signs of a struggle. Annie Mary's little fingers were caked with dried blood from scratching at the inside of the pine box. She had torn clumps of hair from her head, and on her face, where the Twentes should have observed peaceful repose, they saw instead a look of wild terror with eyes wide open. Poor Annie Mary!

Hauntings

Some people say ghosts are the souls of those who have died but haven't crossed over to the other side. Others contend that they are a sort of cosmic movie generated by psychic energy, playing over and over. It is a little spark of electricity that keeps us alive, after all. And it seems little Annie Mary simply couldn't rest.

After the Twentes brought Annie Mary home, they reburied her on the hill, and her father built a four-foot-tall brick wall around the grave, leaving enough room for several more plots within the walls. It's not clear how long after Annie Mary was buried that people began noticing strange things, but neighbors began reporting the presence of a little girl, dressed in white, playing at the grave site.

Years later, cars passing by would occasionally experience electrical problems or their headlights might fail. Some cars stopped running altogether for several minutes. Word about the haunting traveled, and generations of youngsters from nearby communities have made the trip to the Twente farm, trying to catch a glimpse of the ghost of little Annie Mary.

My friend Terry from New Ulm confessed to me that he used to take his dates to Annie Mary's grave, where he could count on the girls to instinctively cling to him for safety. Huh.

BURIED ONE LAST TIME

But Annie Mary was not to be at rest yet. In October 1996, little Annie Mary was disinterred and moved for one last time to a plot alongside her parents at a cemetery in northern Minnesota. The child was even given a new casket. The brick wall surrounding the grave has since been dismantled and the land turned for crops. And *that*, my friends, is the terrible and fascinating story of our little Annie Mary. Rest in peace, little girl.

Strong Words on Strong Stone at Birch Coulee

By Audrey Kletscher Helbling

Westbound on Minnesota Highway 19, I spot the spires poking through the trees high atop the bluffs just outside of Morton in Renville County. But how, I wonder, do we get there?

No sign. No directions, except knowing that my husband and I must drive north to reach these Dakota Conflict monuments.

Now we are already in Morton, and I suspect we have missed the turn. Yet I am determined. I roll down my car window and ask the man walking toward his well-kept brick house for directions. Down a block and to the right, follow the road up the hill, fork to the left, he points.

We follow his instructions and then see the weathered wooden sign, "Historical Monuments," with an arrow pointing east. Soon we are winding our car along a narrow dirt lane edged by trees. Nearly to the top of the hill, we skirt under a fallen cottonwood limb looming over the roadway.

And then we are there, in this stand of oaks, gazing at the two fifty-two-foot-high granite towers: the Birch Coulee Monument honoring fallen soldiers and citizens to our right, the Loyal Indian Monument to our left.

Both recognize those lost in the battle at Birch Coulee on September 2 and 3 during the 1862 Dakota Conflict. I learn later while researching the subject that the fight between white men and Native Americans occurred not on this exact spot but some distance away.

Even here, though, the spirits of those who died at Birch Coulee seem present—in the rush of the wind through the trees, in the solace of this secluded place, in the names etched forever in stone.

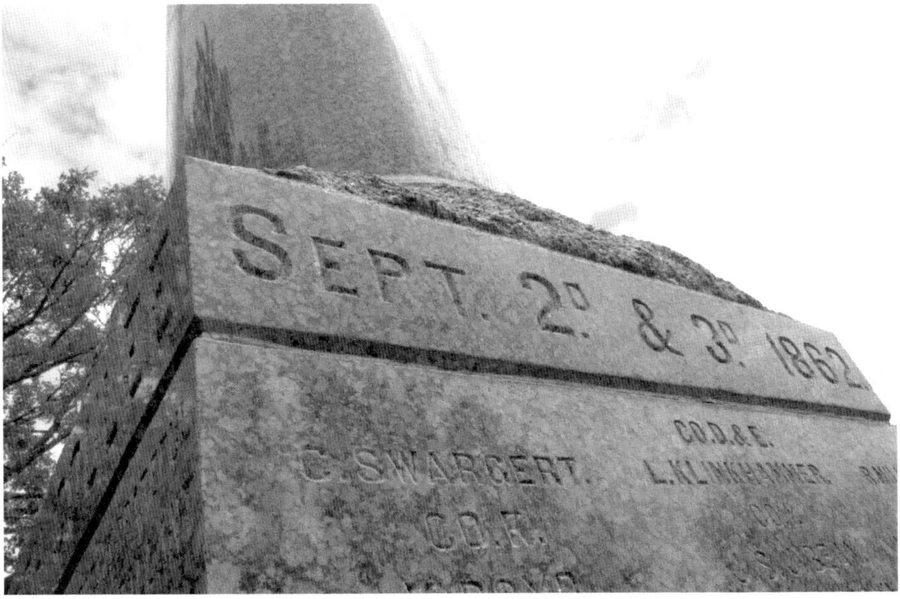

Birch Coulee Monument near Morton, Minnesota. *Photo courtesy of Audrey Kletscher Helbling, Faribault, Minnesota.*

"Erected by the State of Minnesota in grateful remembrance of the heroism of those gallant soldiers and citizens who fought the Battle of Birch Coulee and to perpetuate their names." It is a struggle to read the chiseled words on this multicolored granite memorial placed here in 1894.

Then I walk toward the other monument and see the desecration here in names spray painted upon the stone base. I nearly weep.

"Erected A.D. 1899 by the Minnesota River Valley Historical Society to commemorate the brave, faithful and humane conduct of the loyal Indians who saved the lives of white people and were true to their obligation through out the Sioux War in Minnesota of 1862 and especially to honor the services of those here named," the words read.

It is not lost on me that the tribute to the Dakota—Ampatutokicha, Mahzakutemanne, Mahkahta Heiya-Win and three others—was built five years later than the memorial to the soldiers.

I circle the monument, noting the words, one on each side: Humanity, Patriotism, Fidelity and Courage. Strong words on strong stone.

Later, as we head down the hill toward the highway on a slightly different route, we see the residential street sign, Monument Drive. This, just a plain street sign, directs travelers toward a place honoring those who died nearly 150 years ago upon the land, in a place called Birch Coulee.

The Minnesota River Valley National Scenic Byway

The Minnesota River Valley Scenic Byway was fully designated in 1996 and runs across southern Minnesota from Browns Valley to Belle Plaine.

The river is a tributary of the Mississippi, originating at Big Stone Lake near the South Dakota border and meeting up with the Mississippi at Fort Snelling in the Twin Cities of Minneapolis and St. Paul.

The Minnesota River Valley appeals to a wide range of visitors, thanks to a splendid mix of historical sites, coffeehouses, specialty shops and casinos. Its people are colorful and its history mysterious and volatile.

The byway is a mix of blacktop and primitive roads winding past markers and monuments recording the U.S.-Dakota Conflict of 1862. It is a trip recommended for all members of the family. Visit www.mnrivervalley.com.

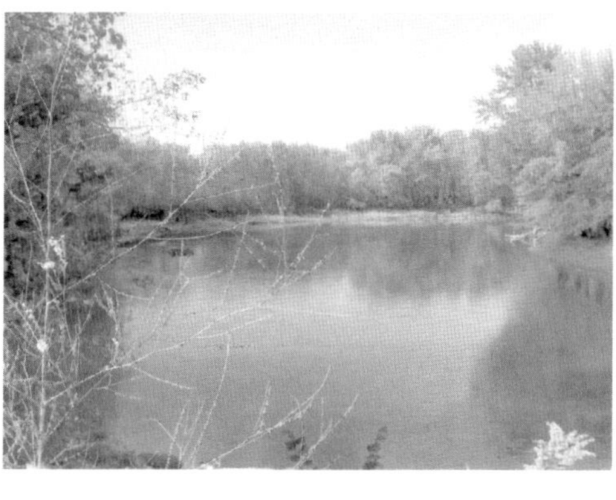

The Minnesota River Valley.

Timeline of Events Related to the History of the Minnesota River Valley

1492

On March 31, 1492, King Ferdinand and Queen Isabella of Spain issued the Alhambra Decree expelling Jews from Spain, an action following closely on the heels of the Muslim Moors surrendering the Iberian Peninsula to them. The Muslim and Jewish land was seized and sold, providing a good deal of the funding for Christopher Columbus's adventure to the American continent.

Columbus, intending to chart a shortcut to the Indies, accidentally winds up on the shores of the New World, mistaking it for East Asia—an accident responsible for the indigenous people of North America being referred to as "Indians."

He wrote of these peaceful people, "They could easily be commanded and made to work, to sow and to do whatever might be needed, to build towns and be taught to wear clothes and adopt our ways." He also wrote, "They are the best people in the world and above all the gentlest."

1524

The first recorded kidnapping takes place when explorers capture a Native American child to take to France as a New World oddity.

1542

"New Laws" are imposed on Spanish colonies ending the right for settlers to force Native Americans into slave labor.

1546
The "New Laws" prohibiting Native American slave labor are repealed, allowing New World colonists to develop a society and economy based on slave labor and cotton.

1600s
European settlers in the New World believed that the diseases they introduced to North America were acts of God provided for their own benefit and not related to the terror they inflicted on the indigenous people. "Their enterprise failed," one settler stated, "for it pleased God to effect these Indians with such a deadly sickness, that out of every 1000, over 950 of them had died, and many of them lay rotting above the ground for lack of burial."

1607
The Jamestown Colony in Virginia was established by the London Company. The colonists suffered starvation, and only a little over a quarter of them survived that year. On July 3, the local indigenous people humanely provided the colony with meat and produce.

1611
A Dutch lawyer by the name of Adrian Block explored Manhattan Island and collected bounty to return home with two kidnapped Native Americans he named Orson and Valentine.

1616
The Native American population in New England is wiped out by a smallpox epidemic.

1626
A Dutch colonist named Peter DeMint takes advantage of the language barrier and purchases Manhattan Island from the local tribe for about twenty-four dollars. He renames it New Amsterdam.

1637
The colonists of Massachusetts are unsuccessful at getting members of the local tribe to cooperate as slaves, so they are sent to the Bermudas in exchange for native Bermudans, who, it was hoped, would be easier to manage. The exchange of Native Americans for black slaves continues for years.

1709
A slavery trade market is established on Wall Street, where black and Native American men, women and children are sold as property of white colonists.

1756
The Scalp Act is declared by Governor Robert Morris, thereby putting a bounty on the heads of all Native American men, women and children.

1804
The Sioux meet Lewis and Clark, and trading posts become established. On March 26, the United States government orders all Native Americans to move west of the Mississippi River.

1820
Twenty thousand Native Americans are living as slaves in California missions.

1823
The Supreme Court decides that titles for land obtained by private individuals from Native Americans between 1773 and 1775 must be turned over to the U.S. government. The government holds title to all native lands based on the Doctrine of Discovery; therefore, making a "discovery" entitled the land to whichever government claimed it. This decision removed the ability for the Native Americans to have a sovereign nation or sell their property at will.

1830
The Indian Removal Act is enacted on April 7 by President Andrew Jackson, forcing all Native Americans to be removed from east of the Mississippi River to west of it. For ten years after that, thousands of natives are forcibly driven from their homes.

1838
In spite of a Supreme Court ruling over seven years earlier allowing the Cherokee to stay on their lands, President Andrew Jackson sends federal troops to forcibly remove them. Sixteen thousand are herded into camps, where they are forced to stay for the summer. Those who survive disease are forced to march eight hundred miles in the fall. Almost four thousand men, women and children died during the Trail of Tears.

1850–1875

Twenty million buffalo, a major food source for the tribes, are exterminated through white men's sports.

1851

On August 5, Chief Little Crow reluctantly signs a treaty at Traverse de Sioux in St. Peter, Minnesota, ceding most of his people's land to the U.S. government. The agreement includes shipments of food and payments of annuities for his people.

1862

Congress passes the Homestead Act, making lands belonging to the Indian nations available for white settlers and setting off a mass immigration west.

The largest mass execution in the history of the country takes place when thirty-eight Native Americans are hanged after the U.S.-Dakota Conflict.

1913

The North American Indians sign the Declaration of Allegiance to the Government of the United States. This document marked the beginning of a ten-year movement to grant full citizenship rights to the American Indians finally given by the Act of Congress on June 15, 1924.

About the Author

Beth Johanneck was born a Minnesota farmer's daughter, with seven brothers and a fabulous sister, and raised on a farm near the tiny community of Wabasso. During her childhood, she was inspired by her mother's creativity and her father's gift for storytelling. She received a bachelor's degree in business from Southwest State University in Marshall, Minnesota, and grabbed an opportunity to work for a tourism office within the central part of the Minnesota River Valley.

She currently resides in the Twin Cities but hasn't forgotten her rural roots, publishing a blog called the Minnesota Country Mouse Folk Blog, where the "hayseed" in her writing betrays her "city-slicker" aspirations. She subscribes to the *early to bed, early to rise* philosophy, celebrating the wee hours of the morning in her big chair with a stout cup of coffee and her computer.